"After utilizing toolkits from The Art of Service, I was able to identify threats within my organization to which I was completely unaware. Using my team's knowledge as a competitive advantage, we now have superior systems that save time and energy."

"As a new Chief Technology Officer, I was feeling unprepared and inadequate to be successful in my role. I ordered an IT toolkit Sunday night and was prepared Monday morning to shed light on areas of improvement within my organization. I no longer felt overwhelmed and intimidated, I was excited to share what I had learned."

"I used the questionnaires to interview members of my team. I never knew how many insights we could produce collectively with our internal knowledge."

"I usually work until at least 8pm on weeknights. The Art of Service questionnaire saved me so much time and worry that Thursday night I attended my son's soccer game without sacrificing my professional obligations."

"After purchasing The Art of Service toolkit, I was able to identify areas where my company was not in compliance that could have put my job at risk. I looked like a hero when I proactively educated my team on the risks and presented a solid solution."

"I spent months shopping for an external consultant before realizing that The Art of Service would allow my team to consult themselves! Not only did we save time not catching a consultant up to speed, we were able to keep our company information and industry secrets confidential."

"Everyday there are new regulations and processes in my industry. The Art of Service toolkit has kept me ahead by using AI technology to constantly update the toolkits and address emerging needs."

"I customized The Art of Service toolkit to focus specifically on the concerns of my role and industry. I didn't have to waste time with a generic self-help book that wasn't tailored to my exact situation."

"Many of our competitors have asked us about our secret sauce. When I tell them it's the knowledge we have in-house, they never believe me. Little do they know The Art of Service toolkits are working behind the scenes."

"One of my friends hired a consultant who used the knowledge gained working with his company to advise their competitor. Talk about a competitive disadvantage! The Art of Service allowed us to keep our knowledge from walking out the door along with a huge portion of our budget in consulting fees."

"Honestly, I didn't know what I didn't know. Before purchasing The Art of Service, I didn't realize how many areas of my business needed to be refreshed and improved. I am so relieved The Art of Service was there to highlight our blind spots."

"Before The Art of Service, I waited eagerly for consulting company reports to come out each month. These reports kept us up to speed but provided little value because they put our competitors on the same playing field. With The Art of Service, we have uncovered unique insights to drive our business forward."

"Instead of investing extensive resources into an external consultant, we can spend more of our budget towards pursuing our company goals and objectives…while also spending a little more on corporate holiday parties."

"The risk of our competitors getting ahead has been mitigated because The Art of Service has provided us with a 360-degree view of threats within our organization before they even arise."

ISO 26262
Complete Self-Assessment Guide

Table of Contents

About The Art of Service

The Art of Service, Business Process Architects since 2000, is dedicated to helping stakeholders achieve excellence.

Defining, designing, creating, and implementing a process to solve a stakeholders challenge or meet an objective is the most valuable role… In EVERY group, company, organization and department.

Unless you're talking a one-time, single-use project, there should be a process. Whether that process is managed and implemented by humans, AI, or a combination of the two, it needs to be designed by someone with a complex enough perspective to ask the right questions.

Someone capable of asking the right questions and step back and say, 'What are we really trying to accomplish here? And is there a different way to look at it?'

With The Art of Service's Self-Assessments, we empower people who can do just that — whether their title is marketer, entrepreneur, manager, salesperson, consultant, Business Process Manager, executive assistant, IT Manager, CIO etc... —they are the people who rule the future. They are people who watch the process as it happens, and ask the right questions to make the process work better.

Contact us when you need any support with this Self-Assessment and any help with templates, blue-prints and examples of standard documents you might need:

https://theartofservice.com
support@theartofservice.com

Included Resources - how to access

Included with your purchase of the book is the ISO 26262

Self-Assessment Spreadsheet Dashboard which contains all questions and Self-Assessment areas and auto-generates insights, graphs, and project RACI planning - all with examples to get you started right away.

How? Simply send an email to
access@theartofservice.com
with this books' title in the subject to get the ISO 26262 Self Assessment Tool right away.

The auto reply will guide you further, you will then receive the following contents with New and Updated specific criteria:

- The latest quick edition of the book in PDF

- The latest complete edition of the book in PDF, which criteria correspond to the criteria in...

- The Self-Assessment Excel Dashboard, and...

- Example pre-filled Self-Assessment Excel Dashboard to get familiar with results generation

- In-depth specific Checklists covering the topic

- Project management checklists and templates to assist with implementation

Purpose of this Self-Assessment

This Self-Assessment has been developed to improve understanding of the requirements and elements of ISO 26262, based on best practices and standards in business process architecture, design and quality management.

It is designed to allow for a rapid Self-Assessment to determine how closely existing management practices and procedures correspond to the elements of the Self-Assessment.

The criteria of requirements and elements of ISO 26262 have been rephrased in the format of a Self-Assessment questionnaire, with a seven-criterion scoring system, as explained in this document.

In this format, even with limited background knowledge of ISO 26262, a manager can quickly review existing operations to determine how they measure up to the standards. This in turn can serve as the starting point of a 'gap analysis' to identify management tools or system elements that might usefully be implemented in the organization to help improve overall performance.

How to use the Self-Assessment

On the following pages are a series of questions to identify to what extent your ISO 26262 initiative is complete in comparison to the requirements set in standards.

To facilitate answering the questions, there is a space in front of each question to enter a score on a scale of '1' to '5'.

1 Strongly Disagree

2 Disagree

3 Neutral

4 Agree

5 Strongly Agree

Read the question and rate it with the following in front of mind:

'In my belief, the answer to this question is clearly defined'.

There are two ways in which you can choose to interpret this statement;
1. how aware are you that the answer to the question is clearly defined
2. for more in-depth analysis you can choose to gather evidence and confirm the answer to the question. This obviously will take more time, most Self-Assessment users opt for the first way to interpret the question and dig deeper later on based on the outcome of the overall Self-Assessment.

A score of '1' would mean that the answer is not clear at all, where a '5' would mean the answer is crystal clear and defined. Leave emtpy when the question is not applicable

or you don't want to answer it, you can skip it without affecting your score. Write your score in the space provided.

After you have responded to all the appropriate statements in each section, compute your average score for that section, using the formula provided, and round to the nearest tenth. Then transfer to the corresponding spoke in the ISO 26262 Scorecard on the second next page of the Self-Assessment.

Your completed ISO 26262 Scorecard will give you a clear presentation of which ISO 26262 areas need attention.

ISO 26262
Scorecard Example

Example of how the finalized Scorecard can look like:

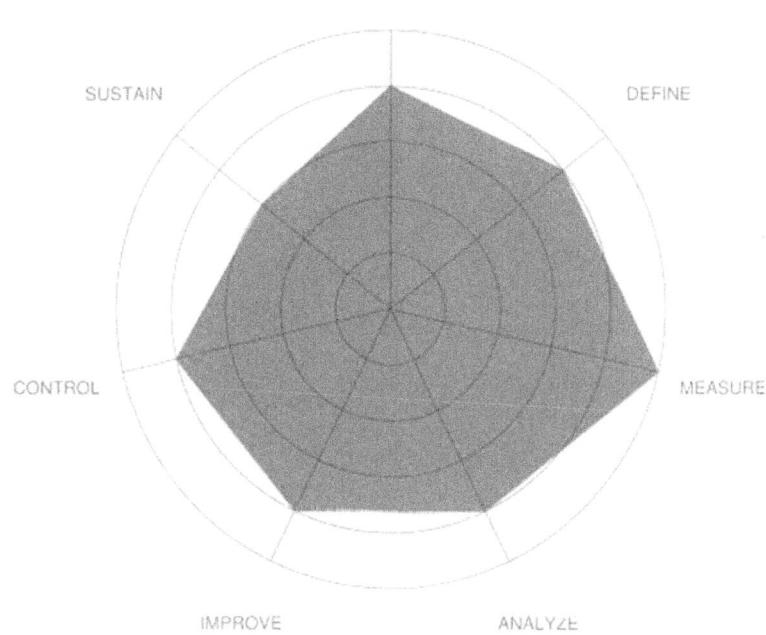

ISO 26262
Scorecard

Your Scores:

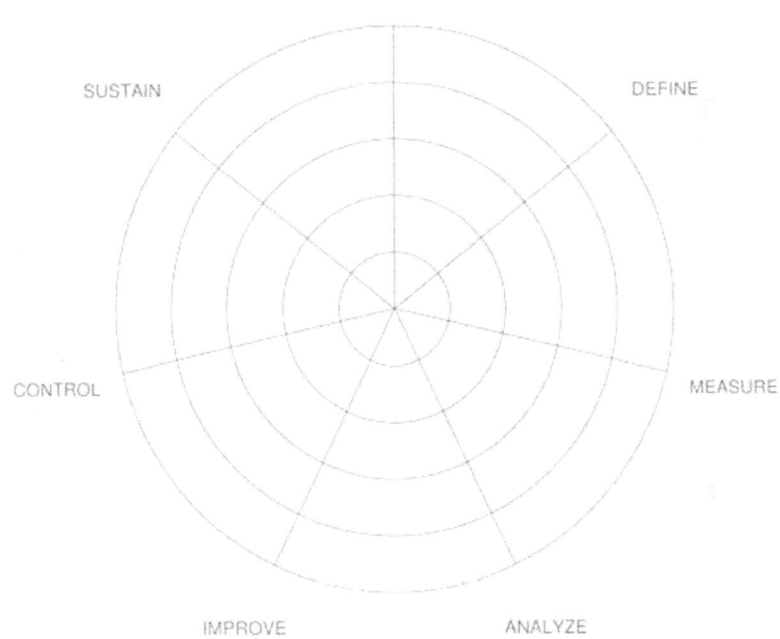

BEGINNING OF THE SELF-ASSESSMENT:

CRITERION #1: RECOGNIZE

INTENT: Be aware of the need for
change. Recognize that there is an
unfavorable variation, problem or
symptom.

In my belief, the answer to this
question is clearly defined:

5 Strongly Agree

4 Agree

3 Neutral

2 Disagree

1 Strongly Disagree

**1. How do functional safety issues change while
going to a new generation?**
<--- Score

2. Who else hopes to benefit from it?
<--- Score

3. Is vehicle delay causing a safety problem?
<--- Score

4. Have you covered the issues relating to safe vehicles accurately and comprehensively?
<--- Score

5. What activities does the governance board need to consider?
<--- Score

6. As a sponsor, customer or management, how important is it to meet goals, objectives?
<--- Score

7. What is the smallest subset of the problem you can usefully solve?
<--- Score

8. What situation(s) led to this ISO 26262 Self Assessment?
<--- Score

9. Does the safety mechanism prevent the failure mode from violating the safety goal?
<--- Score

10. Have the requirements that can affect safety been identified?
<--- Score

11. Are controls defined to recognize and contain problems?
<--- Score

12. Will a response program recognize when a crisis occurs and provide some level of response?
<--- Score

13. What tools and technologies are needed for a custom ISO 26262 project?
<--- Score

14. Act/Adjust: What Do you Need to Do Differently?
<--- Score

15. Are there any potential regulatory or safety issues that need to be considered?
<--- Score

16. What resources or support might you need?
<--- Score

17. What would happen if ISO 26262 weren't done?
<--- Score

18. Consider your own ISO 26262 project, what types of organizational problems do you think might be causing or affecting your problem, based on the work done so far?
<--- Score

19. Do you need an additional layer of thread safety?
<--- Score

20. What are the expected benefits of ISO 26262 to the stakeholder?
<--- Score

21. Will infrastructure support be needed to enhance the safety and reliability of automated driving products offered by the automotive OEMs?
<--- Score

22. What are the stakeholder objectives to be achieved with ISO 26262?
<--- Score

23. Is it needed?
<--- Score

24. How many components do you need to certify?
<--- Score

25. Does the safety mechanism prevent the failure mode from being latent?
<--- Score

26. Will it solve real problems?
<--- Score

27. What does ISO 26262 success mean to the stakeholders?
<--- Score

28. Do recognition rewards increase reuse in your organization?
<--- Score

29. Does the basic safety message need to be changed to deal with articulated vehicles?
<--- Score

30. Have additional safety measures been identified?
<--- Score

31. Who should resolve the ISO 26262 issues?
<--- Score

32. Do you need to change perspectives on safety?
<--- Score

33. How much are sponsors, customers, partners, stakeholders involved in ISO 26262? In other words, what are the risks, if ISO 26262 does not deliver successfully?
<--- Score

34. What actions are needed to achieve the required integrity of functional safety?
<--- Score

35. Are there recognized ISO 26262 problems?
<--- Score

36. Is the agile training needed, or mostly a formality?
<--- Score

37. Are safety and security in industrial systems antagonistic or complementary issues?
<--- Score

38. What are the minority interests and what amount of minority interests can be recognized?
<--- Score

39. How do you identify the safety areas of greater concern or need?
<--- Score

40. How are you going to measure success?
<--- Score

41. How are training requirements identified?
<--- Score

42. Are there any specific expectations or concerns about the ISO 26262 team, ISO 26262 itself?
<--- Score

43. Are safety devices sufficient to prevent vehicles moving during loading/unloading?
<--- Score

44. Do you know what you need to know about ISO 26262?
<--- Score

45. How do you assess your ISO 26262 workforce capability and capacity needs, including skills, competencies, and staffing levels?
<--- Score

46. Have you identified your ISO 26262 key performance indicators?
<--- Score

47. Where do you need to exercise leadership?
<--- Score

48. Why is functional safety needed?
<--- Score

49. Do you need to avoid or amend any ISO 26262 activities?
<--- Score

50. When conducting requirements based testing, what is the problem when requirements are very

detailed?

<--- Score

51. Where is training needed?

<--- Score

52. Is a safe work procedure needed?

<--- Score

53. How often does the system need to catch it and get to a safe situation?

<--- Score

54. What prevents you from making the changes you know will make you a more effective ISO 26262 leader?

<--- Score

55. Is each reliability and safety requirement individually identified?

<--- Score

56. Which information does the ISO 26262 business case need to include?

<--- Score

57. How are the ISO 26262's objectives aligned to the group's overall stakeholder strategy?

<--- Score

58. How to identify key characteristics in manufacturing that are critical to safety?

<--- Score

59. What ISO 26262 coordination do you need?

<--- Score

60. What strategies do current vehicles have for activating a fail safe mode when critical problems are detected?
<--- Score

61. What is the role of silicon vendors to help the security fragmentation problem?
<--- Score

62. Will ISO 26262 deliverables need to be tested and, if so, by whom?
<--- Score

63. What are the ISO 26262 resources needed?
<--- Score

64. What problems are you facing and how do you consider ISO 26262 will circumvent those obstacles?
<--- Score

65. Who needs reliable embedded systems?
<--- Score

66. What determines the activities needed for a modification of a previous product?
<--- Score

67. What ISO 26262 capabilities do you need?
<--- Score

68. How does it fit into your organizational needs and tasks?
<--- Score

69. What should be considered when identifying

available resources, constraints, and deadlines?
<--- Score

Add up total points for this section:
_ _ _ _ _ = Total points for this section

Divided by: _ _ _ _ _ _ (number of
statements answered) = _ _ _ _ _ _
Average score for this section

Transfer your score to the ISO 26262
Index at the beginning of the Self-
Assessment.

CRITERION #2: DEFINE:

INTENT: Formulate the stakeholder problem. Define the problem, needs and objectives.

In my belief, the answer to this question is clearly defined:

5 Strongly Agree

4 Agree

3 Neutral

2 Disagree

1 Strongly Disagree

1. What are the core elements of the ISO 26262 business case?
<--- Score

2. What active transport infrastructure might be required to allow active transport and automated vehicles to interact safely?
<--- Score

3. If substitutes have been appointed, have they been briefed on the ISO 26262 goals and received regular communications as to the progress to date?
<--- Score

4. Is there a ISO 26262 management charter, including stakeholder case, problem and goal statements, scope, milestones, roles and responsibilities, communication plan?
<--- Score

5. Is scope creep really all bad news?
<--- Score

6. Are there any constraints known that bear on the ability to perform ISO 26262 work? How is the team addressing them?
<--- Score

7. What does an assessment require in terms of functional safety?
<--- Score

8. Is a fully trained team formed, supported, and committed to work on the ISO 26262 improvements?
<--- Score

9. What specifically is the problem? Where does it occur? When does it occur? What is its extent?
<--- Score

10. How does the ISO 26262 safety case fit within the existing implicit product safety case?
<--- Score

11. Will team members perform ISO 26262 work when

assigned and in a timely fashion?
<--- Score

12. When are meeting minutes sent out? Who is on the distribution list?
<--- Score

13. Has the ISO 26262 work been fairly and/or equitably divided and delegated among team members who are qualified and capable to perform the work? Has everyone contributed?
<--- Score

14. What are the boundaries of the scope? What is in bounds and what is not? What is the start point? What is the stop point?
<--- Score

15. What are the dynamics of the communication plan?
<--- Score

16. How did the ISO 26262 manager receive input to the development of a ISO 26262 improvement plan and the estimated completion dates/times of each activity?
<--- Score

17. Is the ISO 26262 scope manageable?
<--- Score

18. When is/was the ISO 26262 start date?
<--- Score

19. Has the direction changed at all during the course of ISO 26262? If so, when did it change and why?

<--- Score

20. What are the tasks and definitions?
<--- Score

21. Which evidence indicates that the requirements are complete and correct?
<--- Score

22. How to define/specify acceptable safety level?
<--- Score

23. What information do you gather?
<--- Score

24. What applications are required in terms of safety?
<--- Score

25. Have software safety requirements been derived from the system design specification?
<--- Score

26. Can the software tool malfunction that it introduces or fails to detect errors of safety requirements?
<--- Score

27. Are the ISO 26262 requirements complete?
<--- Score

28. Are all relevant details considered for the functional safety requirements?
<--- Score

29. Has the improvement team collected the 'voice of

the customer' (obtained feedback – qualitative and quantitative)?
<--- Score

30. Does the team have regular meetings?
<--- Score

31. Is ISO 26262 currently on schedule according to the plan?
<--- Score

32. Is the current 'as is' process being followed? If not, what are the discrepancies?
<--- Score

33. What critical content must be communicated – who, what, when, where, and how?
<--- Score

34. Is ISO 26262 linked to key stakeholder goals and objectives?
<--- Score

35. How is the team tracking and documenting its work?
<--- Score

36. What is requirements engineering in agile project, maybe a bit more distributed?
<--- Score

37. Is there any additional ISO 26262 definition of success?
<--- Score

38. What is out of scope?

<--- Score

39. Will your safety case pass an ISO 26262 assessment?
<--- Score

40. Are requirements correctly implemented in the test object?
<--- Score

41. How do you track the safety aspects beyond the scope of ISO 26262?
<--- Score

42. What is safety in a car context?
<--- Score

43. Are reliability and safety requirements specified for each possible mode of operation?
<--- Score

44. Have been considered in the specification of software safety requirements?
<--- Score

45. How does the ISO 26262 manager ensure against scope creep?
<--- Score

46. How do you handle safety requirements for wires?
<--- Score

47. Has/have the customer(s) been identified?
<--- Score

48. Are there hardware, software, watchdog algorithms, etc. requirements or criteria that would help differentiate algorithm designs that are more secure against cyber attack?
<--- Score

49. Are stakeholder processes mapped?
<--- Score

50. Is full participation by members in regularly held team meetings guaranteed?
<--- Score

51. How do you keep the different kinds of safety related requirements consistent?
<--- Score

52. How will variation in the actual durations of each activity be dealt with to ensure that the expected ISO 26262 results are met?
<--- Score

53. Does the model behave correctly with respect to requirements?
<--- Score

54. What information should you gather?
<--- Score

55. What would be the goal or target for a ISO 26262's improvement team?
<--- Score

56. Is there a completed, verified, and validated high-level 'as is' (not 'should be' or 'could be') stakeholder process map?

<--- Score

57. What is out-of-scope initially?
<--- Score

58. Has a high-level 'as is' process map been completed, verified and validated?
<--- Score

59. Is there a clear ISO 26262 case definition?
<--- Score

60. Are different versions of process maps needed to account for the different types of inputs?
<--- Score

61. What scope do you want your strategy to cover?
<--- Score

62. Are improvement team members fully trained on ISO 26262?
<--- Score

63. Is there regularly 100% attendance at the team meetings? If not, have appointed substitutes attended to preserve cross-functionality and full representation?
<--- Score

64. The political context: who holds power?
<--- Score

65. Is the team sponsored by a champion or stakeholder leader?
<--- Score

66. How often are the team meetings?
<--- Score

67. What are the compelling stakeholder reasons for embarking on ISO 26262?
<--- Score

68. What is especially important in the selection of test design techniques in the context of ISO 26262?
<--- Score

69. Have all basic functions of ISO 26262 been defined?
<--- Score

70. What are the requirements for audit information?
<--- Score

71. Is the ISO 26262 scope complete and appropriately sized?
<--- Score

72. How was the 'as is' process map developed, reviewed, verified and validated?
<--- Score

73. Is data collected and displayed to better understand customer(s) critical needs and requirements.
<--- Score

74. What key stakeholder process output measure(s) does ISO 26262 leverage and how?
<--- Score

75. Is the team equipped with available and reliable resources?
<--- Score

76. Are there different segments of customers?
<--- Score

77. Does the person require vehicle modifications to travel safely?
<--- Score

78. How to handle safety requirements for wires?
<--- Score

79. How should minimum safety requirements be determined for automated driving systems?
<--- Score

80. Is it possible to achieve unambiguous requirements in a context of functional safety and ISO 26262?
<--- Score

81. Has everyone on the team, including the team leaders, been properly trained?
<--- Score

82. What are your measures of safety, and what is the level of safety required?
<--- Score

83. Is the work to date meeting requirements?
<--- Score

84. Is there a critical path to deliver ISO 26262 results?
<--- Score

85. Is the team formed and are team leaders (Coaches and Management Leads) assigned?
<--- Score

86. Will team members regularly document their ISO 26262 work?
<--- Score

87. Are customers identified and high impact areas defined?
<--- Score

88. Are team charters developed?
<--- Score

89. Have the customer needs been translated into specific, measurable requirements? How?
<--- Score

90. What sort of initial information to gather?
<--- Score

91. When is the estimated completion date?
<--- Score

92. How much time do you spend with writing and executing test cases?
<--- Score

93. What ISO 26262 services do you require?
<--- Score

94. What are the rough order estimates on cost savings/opportunities that ISO 26262 brings?
<--- Score

95. What are specific safety requirements?
<--- Score

96. Do the problem and goal statements meet the SMART criteria (specific, measurable, attainable, relevant, and time-bound)?
<--- Score

97. What does functional safety require?
<--- Score

98. Are approval levels defined for contracts and supplements to contracts?
<--- Score

99. What customer feedback methods were used to solicit their input?
<--- Score

100. How do you manage scope?
<--- Score

101. What ISO 26262 requirements should be gathered?
<--- Score

102. What is the definition of success?
<--- Score

103. Is the improvement team aware of the different versions of a process: what they think it is vs. what it actually is vs. what it should be vs. what it could be?
<--- Score

104. What types of vehicles are in the future scope

of ISO 26262?
<--- Score

105. Are task requirements clearly defined?
<--- Score

106. What shall be provided to support the Safety Case?
<--- Score

107. Are there test cases that violate a requirement?
<--- Score

108. Is the authority of the software safety organization defined?
<--- Score

109. Has a team charter been developed and communicated?
<--- Score

110. What knowledge or experience is required?
<--- Score

111. Which safety level does society require to tolerate the use of automated vehicles?
<--- Score

112. Where is the verification of safety requirements executed?
<--- Score

113. Are the reliability and safety requirements, taken as a whole, mutually consistent?
<--- Score

114. How have you defined all ISO 26262 requirements first?
<--- Score

115. Is the team adequately staffed with the desired cross-functionality? If not, what additional resources are available to the team?
<--- Score

116. What are the Roles and Responsibilities for each team member and its leadership? Where is this documented?
<--- Score

117. Are the ISO 26262 requirements testable?
<--- Score

118. Has anyone else (internal or external to the group) attempted to solve this problem or a similar one before? If so, what knowledge can be leveraged from these previous efforts?
<--- Score

119. Are accountability and ownership for ISO 26262 clearly defined?
<--- Score

120. Are customer(s) identified and segmented according to their different needs and requirements?
<--- Score

121. Who are the ISO 26262 improvement team members, including Management Leads and Coaches?
<--- Score

122. What is the context?
<--- Score

123. Are the software safety requirements complete and consistent?
<--- Score

124. What constraints exist that might impact the team?
<--- Score

125. Is there a completed SIPOC representation, describing the Suppliers, Inputs, Process, Outputs, and Customers?
<--- Score

126. What defines best in class?
<--- Score

127. What system do you use for gathering ISO 26262 information?
<--- Score

128. How is safe resumption of control to be defined and catered for?
<--- Score

129. Do you have defined at least one functional safety requirement for a safety goal?
<--- Score

130. Where is the verification of software safety requirements executed?
<--- Score

131. What are the requirements for project independent safety management?
<--- Score

132. Are resources adequate for the scope?
<--- Score

133. How do you keep key subject matter experts in the loop?
<--- Score

134. Has a project plan, Gantt chart, or similar been developed/completed?
<--- Score

135. What are non functional requirements?
<--- Score

136. Who is gathering information?
<--- Score

137. Are required metrics defined, what are they?
<--- Score

138. What sources do you use to gather information for a ISO 26262 study?
<--- Score

139. How to extract work product requirements?
<--- Score

140. Which safety level do humans require before using automated vehicles?
<--- Score

141. Does everyone have the required license

validation to operate vehicles?
<--- Score

142. How will the ISO 26262 team and the group measure complete success of ISO 26262?
<--- Score

143. What intelligence can you gather?
<--- Score

144. What is in scope?
<--- Score

Add up total points for this section:
_ _ _ _ _ = Total points for this section

Divided by: _ _ _ _ _ _ (number of statements answered) = _ _ _ _ _ _
Average score for this section

Transfer your score to the ISO 26262 Index at the beginning of the Self-Assessment.

CRITERION #3: MEASURE:

INTENT: Gather the correct data.
Measure the current performance and
evolution of the situation.

In my belief, the answer to this
question is clearly defined:

5 Strongly Agree

4 Agree

3 Neutral

2 Disagree

1 Strongly Disagree

1. Are high impact defects defined and identified in the stakeholder process?
<--- Score

2. What evidence is there and what is measured?
<--- Score

3. What measurements are being captured?
<--- Score

4. How to prioritize road safety policy measures?
<--- Score

5. When are costs are incurred?
<--- Score

6. How to choose cost effective road safety policies?
<--- Score

7. What can cause a functional failure?
<--- Score

8. Which costs should be taken into account?
<--- Score

9. How did systems get so safe without adequate analysis methods?
<--- Score

10. Where is the cost?
<--- Score

11. How can you reduce costs?
<--- Score

12. How can the functional safety of software be assessed analytically?
<--- Score

13. What is the ISO 26262 business impact?
<--- Score

14. Does failure cause safety problem or potential loss of life?

<--- Score

15. What are the current costs of the ISO 26262 process?
<--- Score

16. What are the agreed upon definitions of the high impact areas, defect(s), unit(s), and opportunities that will figure into the process capability metrics?
<--- Score

17. How does it fit into threat analysis and risk assessment?
<--- Score

18. Who pays the cost?
<--- Score

19. What causes innovation to fail or succeed in your organization?
<--- Score

20. Are the measurements objective?
<--- Score

21. How long to keep data and how to manage retention costs?
<--- Score

22. What are the best, better, or most appropriate techniques for analyzing safety requirements?
<--- Score

23. How can the functional safety analysis of ISO 26262 be applied to a cooperative vehicle system?
<--- Score

24. Was a data collection plan established?
<--- Score

25. What key measures identified indicate the performance of the stakeholder process?
<--- Score

26. Does a method exist for managing each risk that may impact safety?
<--- Score

27. Can you measure the return on analysis?
<--- Score

28. What is the total cost related to deploying ISO 26262, including any consulting or professional services?
<--- Score

29. How to verify and validate all the software?
<--- Score

30. Are priorities for SMS implementation based on identified risks?
<--- Score

31. How to analytically assess the functional safety of software?
<--- Score

32. Is data collected on key measures that were identified?
<--- Score

33. Have measures been taken to ensure safe

access for rescue vehicles?

<--- Score

34. Is data collection planned and executed?

<--- Score

35. How large is the gap between current performance and the customer-specified (goal) performance?

<--- Score

36. Is there a Performance Baseline?

<--- Score

37. How do you verify the authenticity of the data and information used?

<--- Score

38. What hazard analysis methods should your organization consider and why?

<--- Score

39. Does your analysis accurately assess the road safety benefits for each reform option?

<--- Score

40. Does each life cycle phase require a safety analysis?

<--- Score

41. Is a solid data collection plan established that includes measurement systems analysis?

<--- Score

42. How will one quantify the probability of software making mistakes?

<--- Score

43. What users will be impacted?
<--- Score

44. What is threat and operability analysis?
<--- Score

45. How do you mitigate the impact of errors?
<--- Score

46. Are models leveraged for validation and analysis beyond code generation?
<--- Score

47. Has a cost center been established?
<--- Score

48. What does verifying compliance entail?
<--- Score

49. Among the ISO 26262 product and service cost to be estimated, which is considered hardest to estimate?
<--- Score

50. What is functional safety analysis?
<--- Score

51. What other hazard analysis methods should your organization also consider and why?
<--- Score

52. What do you measure and why?
<--- Score

53. Has the effect of possible extra functionality been considered in the safety analysis?

<--- Score

54. How likely is the cause to actually result in the failure mode?

<--- Score

55. How to cause the change?

<--- Score

56. How do you measure variability?

<--- Score

57. Do staff have the necessary skills to collect, analyze, and report data?

<--- Score

58. What will the impact be on safety?

<--- Score

59. How much weight do you put into the result of an analysis?

<--- Score

60. How can you reduce the costs of obtaining inputs?

<--- Score

61. Are there competing ISO 26262 priorities?

<--- Score

62. How will your organization measure success?

<--- Score

63. Have you found any 'ground fruit' or 'low-hanging fruit' for immediate remedies to the gap in

performance?
<--- Score

64. What are the most common root causes?
<--- Score

65. What particular quality tools did the team find helpful in establishing measurements?
<--- Score

66. Are process variation components displayed/ communicated using suitable charts, graphs, plots?
<--- Score

67. What measurements are possible, practicable and meaningful?
<--- Score

68. What causes extra work or rework?
<--- Score

69. What are the direct and indirect costs associated with poor quality for OEMs?
<--- Score

70. Are there harmonized safety analysis parallel to the safety activities?
<--- Score

71. What data was collected (past, present, future/ ongoing)?
<--- Score

72. How much does it cost?
<--- Score

73. Is key measure data collection planned and executed, process variation displayed and communicated and performance baselined?
<--- Score

74. What is an unallowable cost?
<--- Score

75. What is most likely to be the cause of your next accident, serious incident or safety occurrence?
<--- Score

76. Have there been unit tests which are compromised because parameters were wrong?
<--- Score

77. Is it possible to estimate the impact of unanticipated complexity such as wrong or failed assumptions, feedback, etcetera on proposed reforms?
<--- Score

78. Which safety and environmental preliminary measures are being considered?
<--- Score

79. Which will have the most impact on vehicle safety?
<--- Score

80. What has the team done to assure the stability and accuracy of the measurement process?
<--- Score

81. Will heavier and larger vehicles have any impact on road safety?

<--- Score

82. What are the costs of delaying ISO 26262 action?
<--- Score

83. Which ISO 26262 impacts are significant?
<--- Score

84. How do you identify and analyze stakeholders and their interests?
<--- Score

85. Why perform dependent failure analysis?
<--- Score

86. How to predict the safety impact of automated driving?
<--- Score

87. How do you do risk analysis of rare, cascading, catastrophic events?
<--- Score

88. Have the concerns of stakeholders to help identify and define potential barriers been obtained and analyzed?
<--- Score

89. Is long term and short term variability accounted for?
<--- Score

90. What happens if cost savings do not materialize?
<--- Score

91. When is Root Cause Analysis Required?

<--- Score

92. How will you measure success?
<--- Score

93. What tests verify requirements?
<--- Score

94. What are the strategic priorities for this year?
<--- Score

95. How do you verify your resources?
<--- Score

96. What safety impact may result from the introduction of automated driving?
<--- Score

97. What are the costs and benefits?
<--- Score

98. Which stakeholder characteristics are analyzed?
<--- Score

99. Which parts of ISO 26262 are sensible and which parts will just cause overhead?
<--- Score

100. What are the types and number of measures to use?
<--- Score

101. What charts has the team used to display the components of variation in the process?
<--- Score

102. What are your key ISO 26262 indicators that you will measure, analyze and track?
<--- Score

103. Is there any update to the stop sale status of impacted safety recall vehicles?
<--- Score

104. How does cost-to-serve analysis help?
<--- Score

105. What methods are feasible and acceptable to estimate the impact of reforms?
<--- Score

106. Does management have the right priorities among projects?
<--- Score

107. Are there any easy-to-implement alternatives to ISO 26262? Sometimes other solutions are available that do not require the cost implications of a full-blown project?
<--- Score

108. What are the key input variables? What are the key process variables? What are the key output variables?
<--- Score

109. What is the cost of rework?
<--- Score

110. What are the incremental safety impact potential?
<--- Score

111. What are the measures for functional safety?
<--- Score

112. Does your organization systematically track and analyze outcomes related for accountability and quality improvement?
<--- Score

113. Did you tackle the cause or the symptom?
<--- Score

114. Are key measures identified and agreed upon?
<--- Score

115. Is Process Variation Displayed/Communicated?
<--- Score

116. Is there an opportunity to verify requirements?
<--- Score

117. Are the units of measure consistent?
<--- Score

118. Who participated in the data collection for measurements?
<--- Score

Add up total points for this section:
_ _ _ _ _ = Total points for this section

Divided by: _ _ _ _ _ _ (number of statements answered) = _ _ _ _ _ _
Average score for this section

Transfer your score to the ISO 26262

Index at the beginning of the Self-
Assessment.

CRITERION #4: ANALYZE:

INTENT: Analyze causes, assumptions and hypotheses.

In my belief, the answer to this question is clearly defined:

5 Strongly Agree

4 Agree

3 Neutral

2 Disagree

1 Strongly Disagree

1. What are some other approaches to novice driver safety?
<--- Score

2. Is the performance gap determined?
<--- Score

3. Is the suppliers process defined and controlled?
<--- Score

4. Are processes and tools being evolved to meet the application needs?

<--- Score

5. Will the drivers required control actions that fall within normal bounds be sufficient?

<--- Score

6. Does a common software process promote reuse?

<--- Score

7. What types of data do your ISO 26262 indicators require?

<--- Score

8. What else can be done to improve safety for novice drivers?

<--- Score

9. Will the primary effect of failure be obvious to the driver?

<--- Score

10. What has to be changed in order to achieve a ISO 26262 compliant process?

<--- Score

11. What are your best practices for minimizing ISO 26262 project risk, while demonstrating incremental value and quick wins throughout the ISO 26262 project lifecycle?

<--- Score

12. What did the team gain from developing a sub-process map?

<--- Score

13. What qualifications are needed?
<--- Score

14. How do you use ISO 26262 data and information to support organizational decision making and innovation?
<--- Score

15. Was a cause-and-effect diagram used to explore the different types of causes (or sources of variation)?
<--- Score

16. How difficult is it to qualify what ISO 26262 ROI is?
<--- Score

17. Do quality systems drive continuous improvement?
<--- Score

18. How to extract the work products process requirements?
<--- Score

19. What successful thing are you doing today that may be blinding you to new growth opportunities?
<--- Score

20. Does it detect change in data order?
<--- Score

21. What will drive ISO 26262 change?
<--- Score

22. What ISO 26262 data do you gather or use now?

<--- Score

23. How to design systems that really support the driver?
<--- Score

24. What does the data say about the performance of the stakeholder process?
<--- Score

25. How are outputs preserved and protected?
<--- Score

26. What conclusions were drawn from the team's data collection and analysis? How did the team reach these conclusions?
<--- Score

27. What promotes and inhibits performance based safety management of design processes?
<--- Score

28. What methods do you use to gather ISO 26262 data?
<--- Score

29. What is the ISO 26262 Driver?
<--- Score

30. What are the ISO 26262 business drivers?
<--- Score

31. Where is the data coming from to measure compliance?
<--- Score

32. Is it possible to handle safety and security within a common process?

<--- Score

33. Is the ISO 26262 process severely broken such that a re-design is necessary?

<--- Score

34. What are the processes for audit reporting and management?

<--- Score

35. What are the personnel training and qualifications required?

<--- Score

36. How will corresponding data be collected?

<--- Score

37. When should a process be art not science?

<--- Score

38. What tools were used to narrow the list of possible causes?

<--- Score

39. What quality tools were used to get through the analyze phase?

<--- Score

40. What is the cost of poor quality as supported by the team's analysis?

<--- Score

41. What other jobs or tasks affect the performance of the steps in the ISO 26262 process?

<--- Score

42. Can it be assumed that it is always the driver?
<--- Score

43. Did any additional data need to be collected?
<--- Score

44. How can functional safety be integrated into established processes?
<--- Score

45. What are the benefits of separating functional flow from data flow?
<--- Score

46. How will the vehicle recognize that it has encountered conditions where it cannot safely drive itself?
<--- Score

47. Are gaps between current performance and the goal performance identified?
<--- Score

48. What are the best opportunities for value improvement?
<--- Score

49. Is tool qualification necessary?
<--- Score

50. Does your organization currently conduct heavy vehicle driver training?
<--- Score

51. What were the financial benefits resulting from any 'ground fruit or low-hanging fruit' (quick fixes)?
<--- Score

52. Are there additional methods you would include in the software assurance process?
<--- Score

53. What drives the software development workflow?
<--- Score

54. Do all activities based on the process model?
<--- Score

55. What is your organizations system for selecting qualified vendors?
<--- Score

56. Were any designed experiments used to generate additional insight into the data analysis?
<--- Score

57. Was a detailed process map created to amplify critical steps of the 'as is' stakeholder process?
<--- Score

58. Are deviations based on a risk assessment process?
<--- Score

59. Is there any way to speed up the process?
<--- Score

60. What ISO 26262 data should be managed?
<--- Score

61. What ISO 26262 data will be collected?
<--- Score

62. What were the crucial 'moments of truth' on the process map?
<--- Score

63. Have the problem and goal statements been updated to reflect the additional knowledge gained from the analyze phase?
<--- Score

64. Will an appropriate automatic response be available to the driver?
<--- Score

65. Do staff qualifications match your project?
<--- Score

66. What performance based tests, methods, and processes do you use for safety assurance of which types of automotive electronic control systems?
<--- Score

67. Who will facilitate the team and process?
<--- Score

68. Did any value-added analysis or 'lean thinking' take place to identify some of the gaps shown on the 'as is' process map?
<--- Score

69. How was the detailed process map generated, verified, and validated?
<--- Score

70. When was the last time you gave your drivers vehicle a safety check and test drive?
<--- Score

71. What tools were used to generate the list of possible causes?
<--- Score

72. How comprehensive is your organizations vehicle incident data?
<--- Score

73. Is there a convincing argument that no interrupt can destroy safety critical data items?
<--- Score

74. Do your employees have the opportunity to do what they do best everyday?
<--- Score

75. What is the output?
<--- Score

76. Does it make sense using it for process capability determination?
<--- Score

77. How will the change process be managed?
<--- Score

78. What, related to, ISO 26262 processes does your organization outsource?
<--- Score

79. How is ISO 26262 data gathered?

<--- Score

80. How will the data be checked for quality?
<--- Score

81. What are the ISO 26262 design outputs?
<--- Score

82. How is data used for program management and improvement?
<--- Score

83. What output to create?
<--- Score

84. Has the processor software been corrupted?
<--- Score

85. Is data and process analysis, root cause analysis and quantifying the gap/opportunity in place?
<--- Score

86. Are all changes processed correctly?
<--- Score

87. What internal processes need improvement?
<--- Score

88. How can risk management be tied procedurally to process elements?
<--- Score

89. Does eliminating driver error lead to safer outcomes?
<--- Score

90. What does an audit require in terms of functional safety and process conformity?

<--- Score

91. Are safety critical data items identified, with types, units, ranges, and error bounds?

<--- Score

92. What are the revised rough estimates of the financial savings/opportunity for ISO 26262 improvements?

<--- Score

93. How is the data gathered?

<--- Score

94. Were there any improvement opportunities identified from the process analysis?

<--- Score

95. Are all team members qualified for all tasks?

<--- Score

96. Does vehicle driver need to read road signage while datp is engaged?

<--- Score

97. What type of evidence should you require before giving a drivers license to an autonomous vehicle?

<--- Score

98. Were Pareto charts (or similar) used to portray the 'heavy hitters' (or key sources of variation)?

<--- Score

99. What data is gathered?
<--- Score

100. Is the gap/opportunity displayed and communicated in financial terms?
<--- Score

101. Are your outputs consistent?
<--- Score

102. Do you, as a leader, bounce back quickly from setbacks?
<--- Score

103. Have any additional benefits been identified that will result from closing all or most of the gaps?
<--- Score

104. Where can you get qualified talent today?
<--- Score

105. What process improvements will be needed?
<--- Score

106. What systems/processes must you excel at?
<--- Score

107. Has data output been validated?
<--- Score

108. What methods are effective in identifying potential anomalous behavior associated with electronic components, systems, and communications reliably and quickly?
<--- Score

109. How important is vehicle safety in the new vehicle purchase process?
<--- Score

Add up total points for this section:
_ _ _ _ _ = Total points for this section

Divided by: _ _ _ _ _ _ (number of statements answered) = _ _ _ _ _ _
Average score for this section

Transfer your score to the ISO 26262 Index at the beginning of the Self-Assessment.

CRITERION #5: IMPROVE:

INTENT: Develop a practical solution. Innovate, establish and test the solution and to measure the results.

In my belief, the answer to this question is clearly defined:

5 Strongly Agree

4 Agree

3 Neutral

2 Disagree

1 Strongly Disagree

1. Does each development team have a common safety rep?
<--- Score

2. How can a streamlined development of smart, safe and secure vehicles be enabled?
<--- Score

3. Have you achieved ISO 26262 improvements?

<--- Score

4. How are policy decisions made and where?
<--- Score

5. What error proofing will be done to address some of the discrepancies observed in the 'as is' process?
<--- Score

6. How will the group know that the solution worked?
<--- Score

7. Do you agree with the overall need to improve vehicle safety?
<--- Score

8. Is there a small-scale pilot for proposed improvement(s)? What conclusions were drawn from the outcomes of a pilot?
<--- Score

9. Are improved process ('should be') maps modified based on pilot data and analysis?
<--- Score

10. What are the effects of safety improvements?
<--- Score

11. What needs improvement? Why?
<--- Score

12. What tools were used to tap into the creativity and encourage 'outside the box' thinking?
<--- Score

13. Do incidents prompt immediate safety review

via a risk based approach?
<--- Score

14. What current systems have to be understood and/ or changed?
<--- Score

15. Is there a cost/benefit analysis of optimal solution(s)?
<--- Score

16. What safety means to consumers and its role in the purchase decisions?
<--- Score

17. How do you link measurement and risk?
<--- Score

18. What is your current residual risk given the current spec / design / implementation?
<--- Score

19. Who are the ISO 26262 decision-makers?
<--- Score

20. How did you arrive at the determination that testing was sufficient and safety risks were appropriately mitigated?
<--- Score

21. What are the acceptable safe speed and risk levels in different infrastructures?
<--- Score

22. How is continuous improvement applied to risk management?

<--- Score

23. Do vendor agreements bring new compliance risk
?
<--- Score

24. How are ISO 26262 risks managed?
<--- Score

**25. How can design patterns support the
development of functional safety systems?**
<--- Score

**26. What specifies the interfaces between a
manufacturer and supplier in a distributed
development?**
<--- Score

27. Are the risks fully understood, reasonable and
manageable?
<--- Score

28. In the past few months, what is the smallest
change you have made that has had the biggest
positive result? What was it about that small change
that produced the large return?
<--- Score

29. What improvements have been achieved?
<--- Score

**30. Are organization vehicle inspected weekly and
the inspections documented?**
<--- Score

31. Would you develop a ISO 26262 Communication

Strategy?

<--- Score

32. Is a contingency plan established?

<--- Score

33. Is a formal, documented and fully functional safety and health training program in place?

<--- Score

34. What is the magnitude of the improvements?

<--- Score

35. What actually has to improve and by how much?

<--- Score

36. Are possible solutions generated and tested?

<--- Score

37. What are the ISO 26262 security risks?

<--- Score

38. What criteria will you use to assess your ISO 26262 risks?

<--- Score

39. Can the solution be designed and implemented within an acceptable time period?

<--- Score

40. What is the overall risk associated with the failure mode?

<--- Score

41. Risk Identification: What are the possible risk events your organization faces in relation to ISO

26262?
<--- Score

42. How effective are plausibility checks in improving the robustness of application software?
<--- Score

43. How do you measure progress and evaluate training effectiveness?
<--- Score

44. Are risk management tasks balanced centrally and locally?
<--- Score

45. Are the most efficient solutions problem-specific?
<--- Score

46. Is there any other ISO 26262 solution?
<--- Score

47. What tools were most useful during the improve phase?
<--- Score

48. How are oems optimizing software for safety?
<--- Score

49. Who should make the ISO 26262 decisions?
<--- Score

50. Is pilot data collected and analyzed?
<--- Score

51. How does the solution remove the key sources of issues discovered in the analyze phase?

<--- Score

52. Who makes the ISO 26262 decisions in your organization?
<--- Score

53. How concerned should developers be about the safety of the system?
<--- Score

54. How do the design patterns for functional safety system development relate to each other?
<--- Score

55. How do you go about comparing ISO 26262 approaches/solutions?
<--- Score

56. What would an architecture developed according to the principles of ISO 26262 look like?
<--- Score

57. Is the ISO 26262 solution sustainable?
<--- Score

58. What were the underlying assumptions on the cost-benefit analysis?
<--- Score

59. Who manages supplier risk management in your organization?
<--- Score

60. Is the optimal solution selected based on testing and analysis?
<--- Score

61. If you could go back in time five years, what decision would you make differently? What is your best guess as to what decision you're making today you might regret five years from now?
<--- Score

62. Do you combine technical expertise with business knowledge and ISO 26262 Key topics include lifecycles, development approaches, requirements and how to make a business case?
<--- Score

63. Does it provide an approach for risk classification?
<--- Score

64. What lessons, if any, from a pilot were incorporated into the design of the full-scale solution?
<--- Score

65. Are new and improved process ('should be') maps developed?
<--- Score

66. Which measurable, safety related maintenance parameters should be improved?
<--- Score

67. How does functional safety relate to development tools?
<--- Score

68. Do you have the optimal project management team structure?
<--- Score

69. Will a system developed according to ISO 26262 really be safe?

<--- Score

70. Are procedures documented for managing ISO 26262 risks?

<--- Score

71. Should frequencies of incidents be part of a risk assessment or a safety case?

<--- Score

72. Are the most worrisome types of defects – is it really worth the risk of letting bugs go into a shipping product?

<--- Score

73. How can technology improve the balance between safety and efficiency?

<--- Score

74. Were any criteria developed to assist the team in testing and evaluating potential solutions?

<--- Score

75. Did you address safety, risk, equity and environment?

<--- Score

76. What is ISO 26262's impact on utilizing the best solution(s)?

<--- Score

77. Who are the key stakeholders for the ISO 26262 evaluation?

<--- Score

78. What assumptions are made about the solution and approach?
<--- Score

79. Does the functional failure or secondary damage resulting from the functional failure have a direct adverse effect on operating safety?
<--- Score

80. What went well, what should change, what can improve?
<--- Score

81. What does the 'should be' process map/design look like?
<--- Score

82. What communications are necessary to support the implementation of the solution?
<--- Score

83. Was a pilot designed for the proposed solution(s)?
<--- Score

84. Does a good decision guarantee a good outcome?
<--- Score

85. Are system level requirements accessible to development teams?
<--- Score

86. How does the team improve its work?
<--- Score

87. How can you improve performance?
<--- Score

88. How risky is your organization?
<--- Score

89. Are risks associated with vehicle selection understood and addressed in your organizational policy?
<--- Score

90. How do consumers incorporate safety and other attributes in making vehicle purchase decisions?
<--- Score

91. How do you manage ISO 26262 risk?
<--- Score

92. Can you integrate quality management and risk management?
<--- Score

93. Who controls the risk?
<--- Score

94. What is ISO 26262 risk?
<--- Score

95. Are the best solutions selected?
<--- Score

96. Is any ISO 26262 documentation required?
<--- Score

97. Describe the design of the pilot and what tests

were conducted, if any?
<--- Score

98. Do the developed methodology and tool chain support the product development?
<--- Score

99. For decision problems, how do you develop a decision statement?
<--- Score

100. Are the key business and technology risks being managed?
<--- Score

101. Do the developed methods and tools support early verification and validation?
<--- Score

102. When are you finished with development and quality assurance?
<--- Score

103. Are there any constraints (technical, political, cultural, or otherwise) that would inhibit certain solutions?
<--- Score

104. How much progress can really be made in optimizing the user interface without safety guidelines from the government?
<--- Score

105. Who are the ISO 26262 decision makers?
<--- Score

106. Is there a safety risk assessment in place?
<--- Score

107. What attendant changes will need to be made to ensure that the solution is successful?
<--- Score

108. What methods are available to improve traceability of potential electronic control system malfunctions?
<--- Score

109. What alternative responses are available to manage risk?
<--- Score

110. Can it evaluate a safe operational design domain?
<--- Score

111. What is the implementation plan?
<--- Score

112. For estimation problems, how do you develop an estimation statement?
<--- Score

113. Is it possible to apply ISO 26262 directly to the development activities of a verification tool?
<--- Score

114. How will the team or the process owner(s) monitor the implementation plan to see that it is working as intended?
<--- Score

115. How will you recognize and celebrate results?
<--- Score

116. Are you developing embedded systems in compliance with ISO 26262?
<--- Score

117. Can you identify any significant risks or exposures to ISO 26262 third- parties (vendors, service providers, alliance partners etc) that concern you?
<--- Score

118. Is the implementation plan designed?
<--- Score

119. How is knowledge sharing about risk management improved?
<--- Score

120. Is ISO 26262 documentation maintained?
<--- Score

121. What tools were used to evaluate the potential solutions?
<--- Score

122. Risk factors: what are the characteristics of ISO 26262 that make it risky?
<--- Score

123. Have any safety risks been identified?
<--- Score

124. Can advanced controls enable performance and safety improvements beyond simply enabling a new vehicle concept?

<--- Score

125. How did the team generate the list of possible solutions?
<--- Score

126. Is a solution implementation plan established, including schedule/work breakdown structure, resources, risk management plan, cost/budget, and control plan?
<--- Score

127. How will you know when its improved?
<--- Score

128. What is the team's contingency plan for potential problems occurring in implementation?
<--- Score

129. Will access restrictions be permitted to improve safety or operations?
<--- Score

Add up total points for this section:
_ _ _ _ _ = Total points for this section

Divided by: _ _ _ _ _ _ (number of statements answered) = _ _ _ _ _ _
Average score for this section

Transfer your score to the ISO 26262 Index at the beginning of the Self-Assessment.

CRITERION #6: CONTROL:

INTENT: Implement the practical solution. Maintain the performance and correct possible complications.

In my belief, the answer to this question is clearly defined:

5 Strongly Agree

4 Agree

3 Neutral

2 Disagree

1 Strongly Disagree

1. Why combine power management and functional safety hardware monitoring?
<--- Score

2. Are there any common design characteristics that help ensure a minimum level of security from unauthorized access to a vehicles electronic control systems?
<--- Score

3. How is ISO 26262 project cost planned, managed, monitored?

<--- Score

4. Does job training on the documented procedures need to be part of the process team's education and training?

<--- Score

5. Why combine power management & functional safety hardware monitoring?

<--- Score

6. Are documented procedures clear and easy to follow for the operators?

<--- Score

7. What is the ISO 26262 Functional Safety Standard?

<--- Score

8. What is the process for updating the standard?

<--- Score

9. Who will be in control?

<--- Score

10. What key inputs and outputs are being measured on an ongoing basis?

<--- Score

11. What should a safety plan cover?

<--- Score

12. Does the response plan contain a definite closed

loop continual improvement scheme (e.g., plan-do-check-act)?

<--- Score

13. How do controls support value?

<--- Score

14. Are there documented procedures?

<--- Score

15. Is there a standardized process?

<--- Score

16. How do you encourage people to take control and responsibility?

<--- Score

17. Should your organization pursue alternative approaches to categorize and prioritize potential electronic control system hazards and impacts to support new standards?

<--- Score

18. Have new functional safety standards been introduced?

<--- Score

19. What kind of monitor is preferable to use in a verification system?

<--- Score

20. What is the standard for acceptable ISO 26262 performance?

<--- Score

21. What other systems, operations, processes, and

infrastructures (hiring practices, staffing, training, incentives/rewards, metrics/dashboards/scorecards, etc.) need updates, additions, changes, or deletions in order to facilitate knowledge transfer and improvements?
<--- Score

22. Are operating procedures consistent?
<--- Score

23. What other areas of the group might benefit from the ISO 26262 team's improvements, knowledge, and learning?
<--- Score

24. What are the critical parameters to watch?
<--- Score

25. Is a standardized approach possible?
<--- Score

26. Does every vehicle meet current design standards for safety?
<--- Score

27. Is there a documented and implemented monitoring plan?
<--- Score

28. Is there documentation that will support the successful operation of the improvement?
<--- Score

29. Is there a transfer of ownership and knowledge to process owner and process team tasked with the responsibilities.

<--- Score

30. How will new or emerging customer needs/
requirements be checked/communicated to orient
the process toward meeting the new specifications
and continually reducing variation?
<--- Score

31. Are new process steps, standards, and
documentation ingrained into normal operations?
<--- Score

32. How might the group capture best practices and
lessons learned so as to leverage improvements?
<--- Score

**33. How does your organization identify
improvement needs and monitor progress in the
areas of health, safety, and security?**
<--- Score

34. Is there a control plan in place for sustaining
improvements (short and long-term)?
<--- Score

**35. Did you find it easy to interpret the standard in
the beginning?**
<--- Score

**36. What security process standard alternatives
are available?**
<--- Score

37. What are you attempting to measure/monitor?
<--- Score

38. Has the ISO 26262 value of standards been quantified?

<--- Score

39. What other standards are relevant for your organization to consider?

<--- Score

40. How do automated vehicles learn to drive safely?

<--- Score

41. How will input, process, and output variables be checked to detect for sub-optimal conditions?

<--- Score

42. What are functional safety standards?

<--- Score

43. How will the standards shape the industry?

<--- Score

44. Where do ideas that reach policy makers and planners as proposals for ISO 26262 strengthening and reform actually originate?

<--- Score

45. Has the improved process and its steps been standardized?

<--- Score

46. What is the control/monitoring plan?

<--- Score

47. Will any special training be provided for results interpretation?

<--- Score

48. Who establishes the standards of safety within your organization?
<--- Score

49. Who is the ISO 26262 process owner?
<--- Score

50. How will report readings be checked to effectively monitor performance?
<--- Score

51. Why is standard needed for automotive cybersecurity?
<--- Score

52. How controllable is the system if the hazard occur?
<--- Score

53. Is knowledge gained on process shared and institutionalized?
<--- Score

54. When working with the standard, what are you experiencing working well?
<--- Score

55. Why do you work in accordance with standards?
<--- Score

56. What are the impacts of growing use of electronics on automotive system safety and how do you assess the adequacy of existing voluntary

standards?
<--- Score

57. Do you formalize the standards assurance requirements?
<--- Score

58. Is there a recommended audit plan for routine surveillance inspections of ISO 26262's gains?
<--- Score

59. How are you affected by standards?
<--- Score

60. Do you formalize standards assurance requirements?
<--- Score

61. What kind of work products are required to be in compliance to the standard?
<--- Score

62. What quality tools were useful in the control phase?
<--- Score

63. How do you plan on providing proper recognition and disclosure of supporting companies?
<--- Score

64. What verification steps are appropriate to ensure that standards are met?
<--- Score

65. Does a standard permit innovation?
<--- Score

66. What should the next improvement project be that is related to ISO 26262?
<--- Score

67. Are suggested corrective/restorative actions indicated on the response plan for known causes to problems that might surface?
<--- Score

68. How do you establish and deploy modified action plans if circumstances require a shift in plans and rapid execution of new plans?
<--- Score

69. What is the recommended frequency of auditing?
<--- Score

70. How to harmonize with the standard?
<--- Score

71. Are standards fit to be used for your purposes?
<--- Score

72. How to make the safety case in compliance with the standard?
<--- Score

73. Do the viable solutions scale to future needs?
<--- Score

74. Is reporting being used or needed?
<--- Score

75. Is new knowledge gained imbedded in the response plan?

<--- Score

76. Does the ISO 26262 performance meet the customer's requirements?
<--- Score

77. What functional safety standards are you using in your organization?
<--- Score

78. Which sections of the safety standard ISO 26262 must you absolutely keep in mind for your projects?
<--- Score

79. What standards can help define a test regimen?
<--- Score

80. How will the process owner verify improvement in present and future sigma levels, process capabilities?
<--- Score

81. What voluntary industry standards are best able to address safety assurance of electronics control system design for motor vehicles?
<--- Score

82. Do you learn from elsewhere, where safety sells?
<--- Score

83. What should a safety plan capture?
<--- Score

84. How will the day-to-day responsibilities for monitoring and continual improvement be

transferred from the improvement team to the process owner?
<--- Score

85. How will the process owner and team be able to hold the gains?
<--- Score

86. Will your algorithm scale from ten data items to ten million?
<--- Score

87. When working with the standard, what are you experiencing working badly?
<--- Score

88. Is a response plan in place for when the input, process, or output measures indicate an 'out-of-control' condition?
<--- Score

89. Have new or revised work instructions resulted?
<--- Score

90. Who controls critical resources?
<--- Score

91. Does it reflect the key priorities of criticality and safety on the project?
<--- Score

92. Is the ISO 26262 test/monitoring cost justified?
<--- Score

93. Which companies are also effected by the standard?

<--- Score

94. Do indicators, targets and trends appropriately reflect the level and controls of safety?
<--- Score

95. Why are specific security standards needed for automotive?
<--- Score

96. Does a troubleshooting guide exist or is it needed?
<--- Score

97. Does ISO 26262 appropriately measure and monitor risk?
<--- Score

98. What, if any, other software assurance standards have you used?
<--- Score

99. What are the control system design challenges for more advanced forms of vehicle automation?
<--- Score

100. Is a response plan established and deployed?
<--- Score

101. How to deal with the parameter for controllability?
<--- Score

Add up total points for this section:
_ _ _ _ _ = Total points for this section

Divided by: _ _ _ _ _ _ (number of

statements answered) = _ _ _ _ _ _
Average score for this section

Transfer your score to the ISO 26262
Index at the beginning of the Self-
Assessment.

CRITERION #7: SUSTAIN:

INTENT: Retain the benefits.

In my belief, the answer to this
question is clearly defined:

5 Strongly Agree

4 Agree

3 Neutral

2 Disagree

1 Strongly Disagree

1. Do you feel the commercial vehicle industry is engaged adequately in considerations, in order to ensure successful deployment?
<--- Score

2. What tools are subject to configuration management?
<--- Score

3. Has the supplier provided all relevant safety, operation, inspection and testing information?

<--- Score

4. Who do you want your customers to become?
<--- Score

5. How many miles of driving would it take to demonstrate autonomous vehicle reliability?
<--- Score

6. Which maintenance activities are related to functional safety?
<--- Score

7. How do you govern and fulfill your societal responsibilities?
<--- Score

8. What is the reliability/safety consequence of the failure?
<--- Score

9. What you are going to do to affect the numbers?
<--- Score

10. How can the potential safety benefits of automated vehicles be established?
<--- Score

11. How well did safe design principles influence outcome?
<--- Score

12. Is safety equipment on vehicles?
<--- Score

13. What kind of design should be carried out?

<--- Score

14. Are all safety devices functional?
<--- Score

15. Can the new feature be implemented in the scheduled time and with the full promise of quality?
<--- Score

16. Are the adaptation safety goals verified?
<--- Score

17. Is the acceleration higher or lower than expected?
<--- Score

18. What is the lifetime of your product?
<--- Score

19. How do you ensure automated vehicles are safe?
<--- Score

20. Are you responsible for a component with special safety features?
<--- Score

21. Are the implemented functionalities related to your day to day safety related engineering activities?
<--- Score

22. Do safety representatives keep records?
<--- Score

23. What one word do you want to own in the minds of your customers, employees, and partners?
<--- Score

24. Is current vehicle evolution compatible with an autonomous systems revolution?
<--- Score

25. What are the usability implications of ISO 26262 actions?
<--- Score

26. How safe are vehicles and equipment?
<--- Score

27. What is the meaning of functional safety?
<--- Score

28. What is sotif and how does it relate to ISO 26262?
<--- Score

29. Are your mounts loaded by shock loading when vehicle hits a large pothole on the road designed safely?
<--- Score

30. Why should you consider about functional safety?
<--- Score

31. Is there a designated organization safety coordinator?
<--- Score

32. How efficient are your functional safety

projects?
<--- Score

33. Where to start driving from the test?
<--- Score

34. How do you provide a safe environment
-physically and emotionally?
<--- Score

35. What is/was done to mitigate hazards?
<--- Score

36. What is the tipping point for safety?
<--- Score

37. How should safety inspections be altered for automated and connected vehicles?
<--- Score

38. How do you proactively clarify deliverables and ISO 26262 quality expectations?
<--- Score

39. What testing has been done to ensure system intrusion safety?
<--- Score

40. What is the source of the strategies for ISO 26262 strengthening and reform?
<--- Score

41. Does the lead vehicle have to comply with safe travel distances for other vehicles?
<--- Score

42. Is the vehicle clean and safe looking?
<--- Score

43. When should you bother with diagrams?
<--- Score

44. Which is a task for a tester in the safety lifecycle?
<--- Score

45. Were lessons learned captured and communicated?
<--- Score

46. What threat is ISO 26262 addressing?
<--- Score

47. What specific periods are imperative to meet business or safety objectives?
<--- Score

48. Is your product secure from hacking?
<--- Score

49. What are the safety challenges associated with highly automated vehicles?
<--- Score

50. What projects are going on in the organization today, and what resources are those projects using from the resource pools?
<--- Score

51. What does a validation approach entail?
<--- Score

52. Is functional decomposition compatible with information hiding?

<--- Score

53. Do you regularly inspect the safety of your workstation and equipment and provide feedback to your manager?

<--- Score

54. Are vehicle induction procedures a component of your vehicle safety program?

<--- Score

55. If there were zero limitations, what would you do differently?

<--- Score

56. Is your organization/authority for accident investigation functionally independent?

<--- Score

57. Do you think ISO 26262 accomplishes the goals you expect it to accomplish?

<--- Score

58. Who are your customers?

<--- Score

59. Why adhere to ASPICE and ISO 26262?

<--- Score

60. How will traceability for the product lifecycle be done?

<--- Score

61. Why is it important to have senior management

support for a ISO 26262 project?
<--- Score

62. Can you do all this work?
<--- Score

63. Do you know what you are doing? And who do you call if you don't?
<--- Score

64. Are vehicles parked in a safe manner?
<--- Score

65. How can communities ensure safety during the transition?
<--- Score

66. Which test environment should you use?
<--- Score

67. Are managers informed to celebrate safety and reliability behaviour from the employees?
<--- Score

68. What knowledge, skills and characteristics mark a good ISO 26262 project manager?
<--- Score

69. Does programming divided does the programming language affect reuse?
<--- Score

70. What is the benefit of a model based design of embedded system for your organization and industry?
<--- Score

71. Do you want a safety clause or petition clause?
<--- Score

72. How can autosar systems become safe?
<--- Score

73. What is it like to work for you?
<--- Score

74. What failures is it trying to protect?
<--- Score

75. How will you ensure you get what you expected?
<--- Score

76. How is the integrated system tested so that its functioning and functional safety can be verified?
<--- Score

77. What functionally safe design strategies can be implemented for automated vehicle functions?
<--- Score

78. How important is vehicle safety to consumers?
<--- Score

79. Are you satisfied with your current role? If not, what is missing from it?
<--- Score

80. How to design the safe, intuitive interaction of automated vehicles with other road users?
<--- Score

81. What is a reliable embedded system?

<--- Score

82. Where are naturalgas vehicles most popular and most numerous?
<--- Score

83. Can an error occur in the product?
<--- Score

84. What are the business goals ISO 26262 is aiming to achieve?
<--- Score

85. Have you participated in a project that was aiming to ensure functional safety?
<--- Score

86. What are the advantages and disadvantages of complying with ISO 26262?
<--- Score

87. In retrospect, of the projects that you pulled the plug on, what percent do you wish had been allowed to keep going, and what percent do you wish had ended earlier?
<--- Score

88. What other parts of the software are affected by that?
<--- Score

89. Do you use AUTOSAR and meet ISO 26262 at the same time?
<--- Score

90. Is your competition venue reviewed for safety

before each training session and competition?
<--- Score

91. What new services of functionality will be implemented next with ISO 26262 ?
<--- Score

92. What is your ISO 26262 strategy?
<--- Score

93. Why is the ISO 26262 necessary at all?
<--- Score

94. What new strategies are employers and workers comp payers using to safely return injured workers to the workplace?
<--- Score

95. Why was the safety operating system the first product to be certified?
<--- Score

96. Which of your work tasks are related to functional safety?
<--- Score

97. Who is vehicle safety more important to?
<--- Score

98. Are managers informed to celebrate safety and reliability behaviour from employees?
<--- Score

99. What are the gaps in your knowledge and experience?
<--- Score

100. How do you cope with tools validation and justification?
<--- Score

101. Is the algorithm model complete?
<--- Score

102. Is the responsibility for the safety of the vehicle expected to change during the registration year?
<--- Score

103. Does the combination of a hidden functional failure and one additional failure of a system related or back up function have an adverse effect on operating safety?
<--- Score

104. How do you feel about your own knowledge and skills in safety matters?
<--- Score

105. How do changes affect automotive test?
<--- Score

106. What should a proof of concept or pilot accomplish?
<--- Score

107. Why are fail operational systems necessary?
<--- Score

108. How to test the integrated system so that its functioning and functional safety can be verified?
<--- Score

109. What are the current best practices for implementing functional safety?

<--- Score

110. Is there any existing ISO 26262 governance structure?

<--- Score

111. Who will determine interim and final deadlines?

<--- Score

112. What really lies behind lean management?

<--- Score

113. How to secure connected vehicles from manipulation and threats to guarantee safe operation and protection of goods?

<--- Score

114. Is there space for the largest vehicle to manoeuvre?

<--- Score

115. What is the difference between shared trustworthiness beliefs and team psychological safety?

<--- Score

116. Are point to point resistance, current density, and electromigration simulations on your must do list?

<--- Score

117. Should you worry about functional safety management?

<--- Score

118. What are the unforeseen consequences with respect to road safety?
<--- Score

119. How safe must an autonomous vehicle be to be safe enough?
<--- Score

120. Can your product deliver faulty function?
<--- Score

121. Which parties influence the in service safety of automated vehicles?
<--- Score

122. How do you ensure that your organization has a safety culture?
<--- Score

123. What must you excel at?
<--- Score

124. Do functional and performance meet original mission objectives?
<--- Score

125. How much money you should prepare in order to roll out ISO 26262?
<--- Score

126. What about incomplete training sets?
<--- Score

127. Has a safe work procedure been written?

<--- Score

128. What is next your functionality wish list?
<--- Score

129. Do you have an ISO 26262 compliant workflow?
<--- Score

130. What are the actual or potential safety/ security consequences?
<--- Score

131. How many safety representatives should there be?
<--- Score

132. What is an unauthorized commitment?
<--- Score

133. How effective are cooperative safety & traffic efficiency applications?
<--- Score

134. Do you conduct health and safety inspections/surveys?
<--- Score

135. How to manage functional safety according to ISO 26262 for an existing safety critical system?
<--- Score

136. How to achieve functional safety?
<--- Score

137. What ISO 26262 modifications can you make

work for you?
<--- Score

138. What kind of information must the employer give to a safety representative?
<--- Score

139. How do you know if you are successful?
<--- Score

140. Would you rather sell to knowledgeable and informed customers or to uninformed customers?
<--- Score

141. Do you ever take time to think about your own personal safety?
<--- Score

142. Is your role in your organization related to functional safety?
<--- Score

143. Is functional safety given system level authority?
<--- Score

144. What is automotive functional safety?
<--- Score

145. What dependencies does that test bring?
<--- Score

146. How big is the probability that the error will be found?
<--- Score

147. What is a functional safety system?
<--- Score

148. Are motorized vehicles and mechanized equipment inspected daily or prior to use?
<--- Score

149. Is there a level of safety at which point you would be willing to use a self driving vehicle?
<--- Score

150. How do you validate autonomous vehicles?
<--- Score

151. Who is responsible for ISO 26262?
<--- Score

152. Does the automated vehicle know when it is about to lose the ability to provide safe operation?
<--- Score

153. What is functional safety assessment?
<--- Score

154. How is functional safety in accordance with ISO 26262 achieved?
<--- Score

155. How to you assess the overall safety performance of your organization?
<--- Score

156. How familiar are you with ISO 26262?
<--- Score

157. What are the estimated efforts for complete

conformity with ISO 26262?

<--- Score

158. Is a vin inspection a safety check?

<--- Score

159. How safe are you in a connected vehicle?

<--- Score

160. Is it in an area with safety concerns?

<--- Score

161. Which portion of that workflow is covered by a tool?

<--- Score

162. Have new benefits been realized?

<--- Score

163. What else can a safety representative do?

<--- Score

164. What factors regarding safety should you consider in your role?

<--- Score

165. How likely can the malfunction be?

<--- Score

166. What is the estimated value of the project?

<--- Score

167. Is your automated vehicle safer than you?

<--- Score

168. What are your safety objectives?

<--- Score

169. How do you ensure automated vehicles are safe at first supply?
<--- Score

170. What additional options are necessary for the safe operation of the vehicle?
<--- Score

171. How does the functionality just implemented work?
<--- Score

172. Why is functional safety necessary?
<--- Score

173. What was the last experiment you ran?
<--- Score

174. What is functional safety and why is it important?
<--- Score

175. Are trials of automated vehicles safe?
<--- Score

176. Where is little to do, where is a lot of work?
<--- Score

177. Are vehicles fitted with appropriate security and kept in a safe place overnight?
<--- Score

178. How can functional safety be incorporated in model based product line engineering?

<--- Score

179. How has iso 26262 been successfully implemented?
<--- Score

180. What are the effects of the failure?
<--- Score

181. Do software components always inherit the highest asil?
<--- Score

182. What keys open the door to road safety?
<--- Score

183. How will regulators approve the safety of every new software release?
<--- Score

184. What programming language is used?
<--- Score

185. What is the biggest challenge radar test engineers face?
<--- Score

186. Think of your ISO 26262 project, what are the main functions?
<--- Score

187. Is the safety mechanism functional and appropriate?
<--- Score

188. Is the impact that ISO 26262 has shown?

<--- Score

189. Why is functional safety important?
<--- Score

190. Why work with time triggered systems?
<--- Score

191. What other software units were dependent on the modified code?
<--- Score

192. What about functional safety when crossing the dotted line?
<--- Score

193. How can software updates be delivered to vehicles safely and with ease?
<--- Score

194. Why is ISO 26262 important for you now?
<--- Score

195. Do robot performance and behavioral style affect human trust?
<--- Score

196. What are the origins of ISO 26262?
<--- Score

197. What are the functional safety implications of moving to a centralized architecture?
<--- Score

198. If you got fired and a new hire took your place, what would she do different?

<--- Score

199. What is the purpose and function of the design?
<--- Score

200. What are the primary concerns regarding safety and efficiency, and how can be managed?
<--- Score

201. Why is your cybersecurity so insecure?
<--- Score

202. Who, on the executive team or the board, has spoken to a customer recently?
<--- Score

203. Do you have a health and safety programme?
<--- Score

204. Have benefits been optimized with all key stakeholders?
<--- Score

205. What does it take to be a leader in safety?
<--- Score

206. Do autosar and functional safety rule each other out?
<--- Score

207. What vehicles come onto site and at what times?
<--- Score

208. How do you communicate safely in your

vehicle?
<--- Score

209. What is the total failure rate per used conditions?
<--- Score

210. Is the charger safe to use with modern electronic vehicles?
<--- Score

211. How much continuous vibration can 3D printed test samples withstand?
<--- Score

212. How do you certify functional safety?
<--- Score

213. Are there means to assure that contract employees follow the safety rules of the facility, including safe work practices?
<--- Score

214. Who is on the team?
<--- Score

215. Are you maintaining a past–present–future perspective throughout the ISO 26262 discussion?
<--- Score

216. What is the safety level of automated driving?
<--- Score

217. Is it safe to overtake the vehicle in front?
<--- Score

218. How are concerns going to be addressed and safety be guaranteed?

<--- Score

219. What do we do when new problems arise?

<--- Score

220. Are the criteria for selecting recommendations stated?

<--- Score

221. What are the long-term ISO 26262 goals?

<--- Score

222. What can policymakers do to promote safety?

<--- Score

223. Is the frequency and severity of health and safety incidents reducing over time?

<--- Score

224. What has been done in the functional safety aspect?

<--- Score

225. What are you challenging?

<--- Score

226. How do you start on the path of creating a quality culture?

<--- Score

227. Can an error be ignored in the product?

<--- Score

228. What challenges can the industry expect from

ISO 26262?
<--- Score

229. What, if any, safeguards should be considered to maintain safe and assured operation of a vehicle?
<--- Score

230. How to gain safe vehicle–kerb access?
<--- Score

231. How likely is the hazard to happen?
<--- Score

232. Have you participated in a project that was certified for functional safety?
<--- Score

233. How to efficiently reach unit testing coverage criteria?
<--- Score

234. Who should perform the reviewing of new concepts?
<--- Score

235. When is it safe to pass another vehicle?
<--- Score

236. Is pre market approval the best approach to regulating automated vehicle safety?
<--- Score

237. What happens at your organization when people fail?
<--- Score

238. Why functional safety in automotive?
<--- Score

239. How are test strategies evolving for autonomous vehicles?
<--- Score

240. Why is ISO 26262 important for your business?
<--- Score

241. Did you have any concerns about the safety of your vehicle while the device was installed?
<--- Score

242. Did you feel safe in the vehicle?
<--- Score

243. What types of metrics are available to test a vehicles ability to withstand a cyber attack?
<--- Score

244. What level of functional diversity is appropriate?
<--- Score

245. What are the reasons for using formal methods?
<--- Score

246. Does the object code to be deployed in the ECU implement the design embodied in the model?
<--- Score

247. How do you assess whether vehicles are safe enough to be allowed on the roads?
<--- Score

248. Can functional safety be achieved with a non compliance?
<--- Score

249. What effect has the hermes project had on road safety?
<--- Score

250. How do you weigh as a privacy advocate that ability to have choice versus the safety features?
<--- Score

251. How safe will automated transport systems actually be in practice after own internal failures are accounted for?
<--- Score

252. Who will manage the integration of tools?
<--- Score

253. Why is integration level testing important?
<--- Score

254. How do you motivate a team to build a functional and correct system in a limited time?
<--- Score

255. Is functional safety enough for safety?
<--- Score

256. How should it be applied to achieve functional safety?

<--- Score

257. What is the benefit of a model based design of embedded systems in the car industry?
<--- Score

258. What evidence demonstrates that your organization has a good safety culture?
<--- Score

259. What are the connected vehicle applications for safety?
<--- Score

260. Do engineers know safety philosophy, or safety implementation?
<--- Score

261. How do you construct correct, safe and reliable software?
<--- Score

262. What are your personal philosophies regarding ISO 26262 and how do they influence your work?
<--- Score

263. Does the system in which the component is installed have safety and protection devices?
<--- Score

264. How to address the safe conduct of automated vehicles?
<--- Score

265. Can a safety representative carry out inspections?

<--- Score

266. Who are four people whose careers you have enhanced?
<--- Score

267. Does the vehicle remain intact or does it break into smaller pieces?
<--- Score

268. What methodology should regulators adopt to assess and validate the safety of automated vehicles?
<--- Score

269. What is functional safety in ISO 26262?
<--- Score

270. Is the code accurate and complete?
<--- Score

271. What is safety and security about?
<--- Score

272. Are the safety functions executed correctly?
<--- Score

273. What is functional safety about?
<--- Score

274. How do you create buy-in?
<--- Score

275. Why do automotive functional safety experts worry about automotive systems having increasing autonomy?

<--- Score

276. Are your responses positive or negative?
<--- Score

277. What safety functionality is desired for the platform components?
<--- Score

278. Why should automotive suppliers have the products certified?
<--- Score

279. What effect would the failure have on the end product and the end user?
<--- Score

280. How do you communicate your idea?
<--- Score

281. Who should certify the safety of automated driving systems?
<--- Score

282. How will the best design or product be made?
<--- Score

283. What is a feasible sequencing of reform initiatives over time?
<--- Score

284. How are safety representatives selected and what are is period of office?
<--- Score

285. How does ISO 26262 integrate with other

stakeholder initiatives?
<--- Score

286. How are safety representatives appointed?
<--- Score

287. Who decides when a vehicle is safe enough?
<--- Score

288. How many vehicles come onto site?
<--- Score

289. Where can you break convention?
<--- Score

290. How can equitable access be provided to support relevant safety messages to all road users?
<--- Score

291. Do the aspects of communication and positioning that are challenged by the presence of large vehicles affect application level performance?
<--- Score

292. Who within your organization is responsible for vehicle related safety?
<--- Score

293. How to determine the parameters of automotive fail operational architectures?
<--- Score

294. Are you familiar with functional safety of software based systems?

<--- Score

295. Did you completely test your model?
<--- Score

296. What should you stop doing?
<--- Score

297. What does functional safety management look like on a day to day basis?
<--- Score

298. What is functional safety in accordance with ISO 26262?
<--- Score

299. What are the implications for software design?
<--- Score

300. How can vehicle routes be managed safely?
<--- Score

301. How can programs be verified for safety?
<--- Score

302. What factors influence the efficacy of each safety technique and by how much?
<--- Score

303. What are you trying to prove to yourself, and how might it be hijacking your life and business success?
<--- Score

304. What is your competitive advantage?
<--- Score

305. Whose voice (department, ethnic group, women, older workers, etc) might you have missed hearing from in your company, and how might you amplify this voice to create positive momentum for your business?

<--- Score

306. Do team considerations about clients consider health and safety?

<--- Score

307. Have you certified the functional safety of a software project?

<--- Score

308. What is necessary concerning functional safety management?

<--- Score

309. Is there a set of clear, safety related, maintenance objectives?

<--- Score

310. Are employees who operate vehicles and equipment authorized and properly trained?

<--- Score

311. Can self driving vehicles really be safe?

<--- Score

312. What is the overall business strategy?

<--- Score

313. How to make sure the system is safe?

<--- Score

314. How do you maintain ISO 26262's Integrity?
<--- Score

315. Have you reviewed the safety routine for returning to your vehicle?
<--- Score

316. Is the dock height suitable for the average vehicle expected to use it?
<--- Score

317. What happens if there will be a fault in a transistor?
<--- Score

318. Are all conflict points between vehicles safely managed?
<--- Score

319. Which ISO 26262 goals are the most important?
<--- Score

320. How do you know were doing enough to address safety?
<--- Score

321. How is safety of automated driving assured?
<--- Score

322. Are new benefits received and understood?
<--- Score

323. What are the essentials of internal ISO 26262 management?
<--- Score

324. Which availability periods are appropriate for which software delivery?

<--- Score

325. Is the ISO 26262 organization completing tasks effectively and efficiently?

<--- Score

326. What is the range of capabilities?

<--- Score

Add up total points for this section:
_____ = Total points for this section

Divided by: _____ (number of statements answered) = _____
Average score for this section

Transfer your score to the ISO 26262 Index at the beginning of the Self-Assessment.

ISO 26262 and Managing Projects, Criteria for Project Managers:

1.0 Initiating Process Group: ISO 26262

1. How will it affect me?

2. How should needs be met?

3. What were the challenges that you encountered during the execution of a previous ISO 26262 project that you would not want to repeat?

4. How can you make your needs known?

5. What is the stake of others in your ISO 26262 project?

6. What are the pressing issues of the hour?

7. What is the NEXT thing to do?

8. Were decisions made in a timely manner?

9. Are you just doing busywork to pass the time?

10. Who are the ISO 26262 project stakeholders?

11. At which cmmi level are software processes documented, standardized, and integrated into a standard to-be practiced process for your organization?

12. Are the changes in your ISO 26262 project being formally requested, analyzed, and approved by the appropriate decision makers?

13. Do you understand the quality and control criteria that must be achieved for successful ISO 26262 project completion?

14. Mitigate. what will you do to minimize the impact should the risk event occur?

15. At which stage, in a typical ISO 26262 project do stake holders have maximum influence?

16. Are the ISO 26262 project team and stakeholders meeting regularly and using a meeting agenda and taking notes to accurately document what is being covered and what happened in the weekly meetings?

17. What communication items need improvement?

18. What will you do?

19. Do you know the ISO 26262 projects goal, purpose and objectives?

20. Do you know if the ISO 26262 project requires outside equipment or vendor resources?

1.1 Project Charter: ISO 26262

21. What is in it for you?

22. Pop quiz – which are the same inputs as in the ISO 26262 project charter?

23. If finished, on what date did it finish?

24. What are the assigned resources?

25. Why Outsource?

26. Dependent ISO 26262 projects: what ISO 26262 projects must be underway or completed before this ISO 26262 project can be successful?

27. What metrics could you look at?

28. Are you building in-house ?

29. Who is the ISO 26262 project Manager?

30. Strategic fit: what is the strategic initiative identifier for this ISO 26262 project?

31. Must Have?

32. ISO 26262 project objective statement: what must the ISO 26262 project do?

33. Who manages integration?

34. Name and describe the elements that deal with

providing the detail?

35. Fit with other Products Compliments – Cannibalizes?

36. When?

37. Are there special technology requirements?

38. Will this replace an existing product?

39. Assumptions: what factors, for planning purposes, are you considering to be true?

40. Why have you chosen the aim you have set forth?

1.2 Stakeholder Register: ISO 26262

41. Who are the stakeholders?

42. How should employers make voices heard?

43. How much influence do they have on the ISO 26262 project?

44. What & Why?

45. What opportunities exist to provide communications?

46. What is the power of the stakeholder?

47. Who is managing stakeholder engagement?

48. Who wants to talk about Security?

49. What are the major ISO 26262 project milestones requiring communications or providing communications opportunities?

50. How big is the gap?

51. How will reports be created?

52. Is your organization ready for change?

1.3 Stakeholder Analysis Matrix: ISO 26262

53. How can you fill the need to show progress?

54. Guiding question: what is the issue at stake?

55. Who has the power to influence the outcomes of the work?

56. Is changing technology threatening your organizations position?

57. Tactics: eg, surprise, major contracts?

58. Where are the good opportunities facing your organizations development?

59. What coalitions might build around the issues being tackled?

60. How will the stakeholder directly benefit from the ISO 26262 project and how will this affect the stakeholders motivation?

61. Who will obstruct/hinder the ISO 26262 project if they are not involved?

62. What could your organization improve?

63. Cultural, attitudinal, behavioural?

64. Guiding question: who shall you involve in the

making of the stakeholder map?

65. How can you counter negative efforts?

66. What do people from other organizations see as your organizations weaknesses?

67. Supporters; who are the supporters?

68. Do the stakeholders goals and expectations support or conflict with the ISO 26262 project goals?

69. Are there people who ise voices or interests in the issue may not be heard?

70. Seasonality, weather effects?

71. If you can not fix it, how do you do it differently?

2.0 Planning Process Group: ISO 26262

72. What is a Software Development Life Cycle (SDLC)?

73. ISO 26262 project assessment; why did you do this ISO 26262 project?

74. What type of estimation method are you using?

75. What do they need to know about the ISO 26262 project?

76. Why is it important to determine activity sequencing on ISO 26262 projects?

77. To what extent do the intervention objectives and strategies of the ISO 26262 project respond to your organizations plans?

78. What good practices or successful experiences or transferable examples have been identified?

79. Will the products created live up to the necessary quality?

80. Did the program design/ implementation strategy adequately address the planning stage necessary to set up structures, hire staff etc.?

81. What types of differentiated effects are resulting from the ISO 26262 project and to what extent?

82. If a task is partitionable, is this a sufficient condition to reduce the ISO 26262 project duration?

83. In what ways can the governance of the ISO 26262 project be improved so that it has greater likelihood of achieving future sustainability?

84. Is the identification of the problems, inequalities and gaps, with respective causes, clear in the ISO 26262 project?

85. Mitigate. what will you do to minimize the impact should a risk event occur?

86. If task x starts two days late, what is the effect on the ISO 26262 project end date?

87. How can you tell when you are done?

88. How are it ISO 26262 projects different?

2.1 Project Management Plan: ISO 26262

89. Are cost risk analysis methods applied to develop contingencies for the estimated total ISO 26262 project costs?

90. What does management expect of PMs?

91. Do there need to be organizational changes?

92. What are the training needs?

93. Are alternatives safe, functional, constructible, economical, reasonable and sustainable?

94. Who is the sponsor?

95. Has the selected plan been formulated using cost effectiveness and incremental analysis techniques?

96. What are the deliverables?

97. Does the selected plan protect privacy?

98. What went wrong?

99. Are calculations and results of analyzes essentially correct?

100. Are there any Client staffing expectations?

101. What are the assumptions?

102. What are the constraints?

103. Is there an incremental analysis/cost effectiveness analysis of proposed mitigation features based on an approved method and using an accepted model?

104. Did the planning effort collaborate to develop solutions that integrate expertise, policies, programs, and ISO 26262 projects across entities?

105. Is there anything you would now do differently on your ISO 26262 project based on past experience?

2.2 Scope Management Plan: ISO 26262

106. What problem is being solved by delivering this ISO 26262 project?

107. What is the unique product, service or result?

108. Will your organizations estimating methodology be used and followed?

109. Organizational unit (e.g., department, team, or person) who will accept responsibility for satisfactory completion of the item?

110. Have adequate resources been provided by management to ensure ISO 26262 project success?

111. What strengths do you have?

112. Is your organization structure for both tracking & controlling the budget well defined and assigned to a specific individual?

113. Is there a formal set of procedures supporting Stakeholder Management?

114. Does all ISO 26262 project documentation reside in a common repository for easy access?

115. Is stakeholder involvement adequate?

116. Can the ISO 26262 project team do several

activities in parallel?

117. For which criterion is it tolerable not to meet the original parameters?

118. Is the quality assurance team identified?

119. Has a sponsor been identified?

120. Has the business need been clearly defined?

121. Can each item be appropriately scheduled?

122. Are funding resource estimates sufficiently detailed and documented for use in planning and tracking the ISO 26262 project?

123. Who is responsible for monitoring the ISO 26262 project scope to ensure the ISO 26262 project remains within the scope baseline?

124. Has process improvement efforts been completed before requirements efforts begin?

2.3 Requirements Management Plan: ISO 26262

125. What went right?

126. Did you use declarative statements?

127. Who will initially review the ISO 26262 project work or products to ensure it meets the applicable acceptance criteria?

128. Who is responsible for quantifying the ISO 26262 project requirements?

129. Why manage requirements?

130. How knowledgeable is the team in the proposed application area?

131. How will you develop the schedule of requirements activities?

132. After the requirements are gathered and set forth on the requirements register, theyre little more than a laundry list of items. Some may be duplicates, some might conflict with others and some will be too broad or too vague to understand. Describe how the requirements will be analyzed. Who will perform the analysis?

133. Is the user satisfied?

134. Who will do the reporting and to whom will

reports be delivered?

135. Did you distinguish the scope of work the contractor(s) will be required to do?

136. Will you perform a Requirements Risk assessment and develop a plan to deal with risks?

137. Is there formal agreement on who has authority to request a change in requirements?

138. Business analysis scope?

139. Subject to change control?

140. How will the requirements become prioritized?

141. How will unresolved questions be handled once approval has been obtained?

142. Who has the authority to reject ISO 26262 project requirements?

143. Have stakeholders been instructed in the Change Control process?

144. What information regarding the ISO 26262 project requirements will be reported?

2.4 Requirements Documentation: ISO 26262

145. What are the acceptance criteria?

146. Does your organization restrict technical alternatives?

147. How to document system requirements?

148. Basic work/business process; high-level, what is being touched?

149. What are current process problems?

150. Are there legal issues?

151. What if the system wasn t implemented?

152. What are the potential disadvantages/ advantages?

153. The problem with gathering requirements is right there in the word gathering. What images does it conjure?

154. What is your Elevator Speech?

155. Who is involved?

156. If applicable; are there issues linked with the fact that this is an offshore ISO 26262 project?

157. What happens when requirements are wrong?

158. What images does it conjure?

159. Has requirements gathering uncovered information that would necessitate changes?

160. Where do you define what is a customer, what are the attributes of customer?

161. What is a show stopper in the requirements?

162. Can the requirement be changed without a large impact on other requirements?

163. Is your business case still valid?

164. Can the requirements be checked?

2.5 Requirements Traceability Matrix: ISO 26262

165. Will you use a Requirements Traceability Matrix?

166. What are the chronologies, contingencies, consequences, criteria?

167. How will it affect the stakeholders personally in career?

168. Describe the process for approving requirements so they can be added to the traceability matrix and ISO 26262 project work can be performed. Will the ISO 26262 project requirements become approved in writing?

169. How small is small enough?

170. Is there a requirements traceability process in place?

171. What is the WBS?

172. Why use a WBS?

173. Do you have a clear understanding of all subcontracts in place?

174. Why do you manage scope?

175. What percentage of ISO 26262 projects are producing traceability matrices between

requirements and other work products?

176. How do you manage scope?

2.6 Project Scope Statement: ISO 26262

177. Are the input requirements from the team members clearly documented and communicated?

178. Is your organization structure appropriate for the ISO 26262 projects size and complexity?

179. Which risks does the ISO 26262 project focus on?

180. Is the quality function identified and assigned?

181. What is a process you might recommend to verify the accuracy of the research deliverable?

182. If there are vendors, have they signed off on the ISO 26262 project Plan?

183. Was planning completed before the ISO 26262 project was initiated?

184. If the scope changes, what will the impact be to your ISO 26262 project in terms of duration, cost, quality, or any other important areas of the ISO 26262 project?

185. How often do you estimate that the scope might change, and why?

186. Is an issue management process documented and filed?

187. Is there a Change Management Board?

188. Will statistics related to QA be collected, trends analyzed, and problems raised as issues?

189. What should you drop in order to add something new?

190. Elements that deal with providing the detail?

191. What is the most common tool for helping define the detail?

192. Is there an information system for the ISO 26262 project?

193. Are the meetings set up to have assigned note takers that will add action/issues to the issue list?

194. Are there adequate ISO 26262 project control systems?

195. Is there a process (test plans, inspections, reviews) defined for verifying outputs for each task?

196. Will all tasks resulting from issues be entered into the ISO 26262 project Plan and tracked through the plan?

2.7 Assumption and Constraint Log: ISO 26262

197. Are requirements management tracking tools and procedures in place?

198. Are formal code reviews conducted?

199. When can log be discarded?

200. What if failure during recovery?

201. Contradictory information between different documents?

202. How can you prevent/fix violations?

203. Does the document/deliverable meet general requirements (for example, statement of work) for all deliverables?

204. What would you gain if you spent time working to improve this process?

205. Is there a Steering Committee in place?

206. Can you perform this task or activity in a more effective manner?

207. Do the requirements meet the standards of correctness, completeness, consistency, accuracy, and readability?

208. What worked well?

209. Security analysis has access to information that is sanitized?

210. Does the system design reflect the requirements?

211. Has the approach and development strategy of the ISO 26262 project been defined, documented and accepted by the appropriate stakeholders?

212. How relevant is this attribute to this ISO 26262 project or audit?

213. Contradictory information between document sections?

214. If it is out of compliance, should the process be amended or should the Plan be amended?

215. Is the process working, and people are not executing in compliance of the process?

216. What do you audit?

2.8 Work Breakdown Structure: ISO 26262

217. Where does it take place?

218. How far down?

219. When do you stop?

220. When would you develop a Work Breakdown Structure?

221. What has to be done?

222. Can you make it?

223. Who has to do it?

224. How big is a work-package?

225. How many levels?

226. When does it have to be done?

227. What is the probability that the ISO 26262 project duration will exceed xx weeks?

228. Why is it useful?

229. What is the probability of completing the ISO 26262 project in less that xx days?

230. How will you and your ISO 26262 project team

define the ISO 26262 projects scope and work breakdown structure?

231. How much detail?

232. Do you need another level?

2.9 WBS Dictionary: ISO 26262

233. Are the latest revised estimates of costs at completion compared with the established budgets at appropriate levels and causes of variances identified?

234. Are budgets or values assigned to work packages and planning packages in terms of dollars, hours, or other measurable units?

235. Contemplated overhead expenditure for each period based on the best information currently available?

236. Is each control account assigned to a single organizational element directly responsible for the work and identifiable to a single element of the CWBS?

237. Are time-phased budgets established for planning and control of level of effort activity by category of resource; for example, type of manpower and/or material?

238. Is all contract work included in the CWBS?

239. Budgets assigned to control accounts?

240. Are control accounts opened and closed based on the start and completion of work contained therein?

241. Is authorization of budgets in excess of the

contract budget base controlled formally and done with the full knowledge and recognition of the procuring activity?

242. Are estimates developed by ISO 26262 project personnel coordinated with the already stated responsible for overall management to determine whether required resources will be available according to revised planning?

243. Changes in the current direct and ISO 26262 projected base?

244. Are indirect costs accumulated for comparison with the corresponding budgets?

245. Do procedures specify under what circumstances replanning of open work packages may occur, and the methods to be followed?

246. Is cost performance measurement at the point in time most suitable for the category of material involved, and no earlier than the time of actual receipt of material?

247. Is work progressively subdivided into detailed work packages as requirements are defined?

248. Are overhead costs budgets established on a basis consistent with anticipated direct business base?

249. Are the procedures for identifying indirect costs to incurring organizations, indirect cost pools, and allocating the costs from the pools to the contracts formally documented?

250. Are the contractors estimates of costs at completion reconcilable with cost data reported to us?

251. Do the lines of authority for incurring indirect costs correspond to the lines of responsibility for management control of the same components of costs?

2.10 Schedule Management Plan: ISO 26262

252. Have external dependencies been captured in the schedule?

253. How do you manage time?

254. Sensitivity analysis?

255. What weaknesses do you have?

256. Is the steering committee active in ISO 26262 project oversight?

257. Are procurement deliverables arriving on time and to specification?

258. Are the processes for status updates and maintenance defined?

259. Are corrective actions and variances reported?

260. Is a payment system in place with proper reviews and approvals?

261. Pareto diagrams, statistical sampling, flow charting or trend analysis used quality monitoring?

262. Does the schedule have reasonable float?

263. Is there an excessive and invalid use of task constraints and relationships of leads/lags?

264. Can additional resources be added to subsequent tasks to reduce the durations of the already stated tasks?

265. Was the scope definition used in task sequencing?

266. Is the schedule feasible and at what cost?

267. Are staff skills known and available for each task?

268. Are risk oriented checklists used during risk identification?

269. Are the primary and secondary schedule tools defined?

270. What does a valid Schedule look like?

2.11 Activity List: ISO 26262

271. Can you determine the activity that must finish, before this activity can start?

272. What is your organizations history in doing similar activities?

273. When do the individual activities need to start and finish?

274. What are you counting on?

275. How much slack is available in the ISO 26262 project?

276. Is there anything planned that does not need to be here?

277. How will it be performed?

278. How difficult will it be to do specific activities on this ISO 26262 project?

279. What did not go as well?

280. For other activities, how much delay can be tolerated?

281. How should ongoing costs be monitored to try to keep the ISO 26262 project within budget?

282. What will be performed?

283. What are the critical bottleneck activities?

284. How detailed should a ISO 26262 project get?

285. What is the LF and LS for each activity?

286. How can the ISO 26262 project be displayed graphically to better visualize the activities?

287. Is infrastructure setup part of your ISO 26262 project?

288. Should you include sub-activities?

2.12 Activity Attributes: ISO 26262

289. Activity: what is Missing?

290. Are the required resources available or need to be acquired?

291. How many resources do you need to complete the work scope within a limit of X number of days?

292. What activity do you think you should spend the most time on?

293. How difficult will it be to do specific activities on this ISO 26262 project?

294. Can more resources be added?

295. Where else does it apply?

296. Activity: what is In the Bag?

297. Has management defined a definite timeframe for the turnaround or ISO 26262 project window?

298. Why?

299. Have you identified the Activity Leveling Priority code value on each activity?

300. What is the general pattern here?

301. What is missing?

302. Have constraints been applied to the start and finish milestones for the phases?

303. How else could the items be grouped?

304. Would you consider either of corresponding activities an outlier?

305. Resource is assigned to?

306. How many days do you need to complete the work scope with a limit of X number of resources?

2.13 Milestone List: ISO 26262

307. Calculate how long can activity be delayed?

308. Continuity, supply chain robustness?

309. Loss of key staff?

310. Sustainable financial backing?

311. How soon can the activity finish?

312. Insurmountable weaknesses?

313. Which path is the critical path?

314. Environmental effects?

315. Who will manage the ISO 26262 project on a day-to-day basis?

316. What is the market for your technology, product or service?

317. How soon can the activity start?

318. Global influences?

319. Reliability of data, plan predictability?

320. Timescales, deadlines and pressures?

321. Information and research?

322. How late can the activity start?

323. Own known vulnerabilities?

324. New USPs?

325. Describe your organizations strengths and core competencies. What factors will make your organization succeed?

2.14 Network Diagram: ISO 26262

326. Are you on time?

327. How difficult will it be to do specific activities on this ISO 26262 project?

328. Can you calculate the confidence level?

329. What activities must occur simultaneously with this activity?

330. Why must you schedule milestones, such as reviews, throughout the ISO 26262 project?

331. What controls the start and finish of a job?

332. What is the lowest cost to complete this ISO 26262 project in xx weeks?

333. Where do you schedule uncertainty time?

334. What are the tools?

335. Which type of network diagram allows you to depict four types of dependencies?

336. If x is long, what would be the completion time if you break x into two parallel parts of y weeks and z weeks?

337. If a current contract exists, can you provide the vendor name, contract start, and contract expiration date?

338. Will crashing x weeks return more in benefits than it costs?

339. If the ISO 26262 project network diagram cannot change and you have extra personnel resources, what is the BEST thing to do?

340. Where do schedules come from?

341. How confident can you be in your milestone dates and the delivery date?

342. What to do and When?

343. What can be done concurrently?

344. What job or jobs precede it?

345. What are the Key Success Factors?

2.15 Activity Resource Requirements: ISO 26262

346. Which logical relationship does the PDM use most often?

347. How do you handle petty cash?

348. Organizational Applicability?

349. What are constraints that you might find during the Human Resource Planning process?

350. Do you use tools like decomposition and rolling-wave planning to produce the activity list and other outputs?

351. How many signatures do you require on a check and does this match what is in your policy and procedures?

352. Other support in specific areas?

353. Why do you do that?

354. What is the Work Plan Standard?

355. Time for overtime?

356. Anything else?

357. Are there unresolved issues that need to be addressed?

358. When does monitoring begin?

2.16 Resource Breakdown Structure: ISO 26262

359. Why do you do it?

360. What defines a successful ISO 26262 project?

361. When do they need the information?

362. Why is this important?

363. What is ISO 26262 project communication management?

364. Goals for the ISO 26262 project. What is each stakeholders desired outcome for the ISO 26262 project?

365. Which resources should be in the resource pool?

366. What is the primary purpose of the human resource plan?

367. Who delivers the information?

368. What defines a successful ISO 26262 project?

369. How difficult will it be to do specific activities on this ISO 26262 project?

370. The list could probably go on, but, the thing that you would most like to know is, How long & How much?

371. What can you do to improve productivity?

372. Who will be used as a ISO 26262 project team member?

373. Is predictive resource analysis being done?

374. Who needs what information?

375. What is the number one predictor of a groups productivity?

376. What is the difference between % Complete and % work?

2.17 Activity Duration Estimates: ISO 26262

377. Does a process exist to determine which risk events to accept and which events to disregard?

378. Do scope statements include the ISO 26262 project objectives and expected deliverables?

379. Do procedures exist that identify when and how human resources are introduced and removed from the ISO 26262 project?

380. How does a ISO 26262 project life cycle differ from a product life cycle?

381. If ISO 26262 project time and cost are not as important as the number of resources used each month, which is the BEST thing to do?

382. What are some crucial elements of a good ISO 26262 project plan?

383. It under budget or over budget?

384. Calculate the expected duration for an activity that has a most likely time of 3, a pessimistic time of 10, and a optimiztic time of 2?

385. How does ISO 26262 project integration management relate to the ISO 26262 project life cycle, stakeholders, and the other ISO 26262 project management knowledge areas?

386. What are the main processes included in ISO 26262 project quality management?

387. How can others help ISO 26262 project managers understand your organizational context for ISO 26262 projects?

388. What ISO 26262 project was the first to use modern ISO 26262 project management?

389. Are updates on work results collected and used as inputs to the performance reporting process?

390. Will it help in finding or retaining employees?

391. Are procurement documents used to solicit accurate and complete proposals from prospective sellers?

392. Are contractor costs, schedule and technical performance monitored throughout the ISO 26262 project?

393. Which suggestions do you find most useful?

394. Are ISO 26262 project records organized, maintained, and assessable by ISO 26262 project team members?

2.18 Duration Estimating Worksheet: ISO 26262

395. What is an Average ISO 26262 project?

396. What is your role?

397. How can the ISO 26262 project be displayed graphically to better visualize the activities?

398. Small or large ISO 26262 project?

399. When, then?

400. What work will be included in the ISO 26262 project?

401. Done before proceeding with this activity or what can be done concurrently?

402. Why estimate costs?

403. When does your organization expect to be able to complete it?

404. What utility impacts are there?

405. What info is needed?

406. Is this operation cost effective?

407. Is the ISO 26262 project responsive to community need?

408. Do any colleagues have experience with your organization and/or RFPs?

409. Define the work as completely as possible. What work will be included in the ISO 26262 project?

410. Science = process: remember the scientific method?

411. Can the ISO 26262 project be constructed as planned?

412. Value pocket identification & quantification what are value pockets?

413. What is next?

2.19 Project Schedule: ISO 26262

414. Why is software ISO 26262 project disaster so common?

415. Eliminate unnecessary activities. Are there activities that came from a template or previous ISO 26262 project that are not applicable on this phase of this ISO 26262 project?

416. How effectively were issues able to be resolved without impacting the ISO 26262 project Schedule or Budget?

417. Are all remaining durations correct?

418. If there are any qualifying green components to this ISO 26262 project, what portion of the total ISO 26262 project cost is green?

419. Why do you need to manage ISO 26262 project Risk?

420. How can you fix it?

421. How can slack be negative?

422. Your best shot for providing estimations how complex/how much work does the activity require?

423. How do you manage ISO 26262 project Risk?

424. Why do you need schedules?

425. Are quality inspections and review activities listed in the ISO 26262 project schedule(s)?

426. What is risk?

427. What is the most mis-scheduled part of process?

428. To what degree is do you feel the entire team was committed to the ISO 26262 project schedule?

429. Change management required?

430. Is infrastructure setup part of your ISO 26262 project?

431. Verify that the update is accurate. Are all remaining durations correct?

432. Is ISO 26262 project work proceeding in accordance with the original ISO 26262 project schedule?

2.20 Cost Management Plan: ISO 26262

433. Are the ISO 26262 project plans updated on a frequent basis?

434. Were stakeholders aware and supportive of the principles and practices of modern software estimation?

435. Was the ISO 26262 project schedule reviewed by all stakeholders and formally accepted?

436. Is ISO 26262 project status reviewed with the steering and executive teams at appropriate intervals?

437. Are the people assigned to the ISO 26262 project sufficiently qualified?

438. Have adequate resources been provided by management to ensure ISO 26262 project success?

439. Have all documents been archived in a ISO 26262 project repository for each release?

440. Are changes in deliverable commitments agreed to by all affected groups & individuals?

441. Environmental management – what changes in statutory environmental compliance requirements are anticipated during the ISO 26262 project?

442. Is there any form of automated support for Issues

Management?

443. Are risk triggers captured?

444. Is it a ISO 26262 project?

445. What is cost and ISO 26262 project cost management?

446. Is there an approved case?

447. Have stakeholder accountabilities & responsibilities been clearly defined?

2.21 Activity Cost Estimates: ISO 26262

448. Were the costs or charges reasonable?

449. How do you fund change orders?

450. What areas does the group agree are the biggest success on the ISO 26262 project?

451. What is the estimators estimating history?

452. What makes a good activity description?

453. What is the last item a ISO 26262 project manager must do to finalize ISO 26262 project close-out?

454. What is the activity inventory?

455. What is ISO 26262 project cost management?

456. Were sponsors and decision makers available when needed outside regularly scheduled meetings?

457. How Award?

458. What happens if you cannot produce the documentation for the single audit?

459. What is procurement?

460. How difficult will it be to do specific tasks on the

ISO 26262 project?

461. Are cost subtotals needed?

462. Who determines when the contractor is paid?

463. Are data needed on characteristics of care?

464. How do you allocate indirect costs to activities?

465. What were things that you did very well and want to do the same again on the next ISO 26262 project?

466. Specific - is the objective clear in terms of what, how, when, and where the situation will be changed?

2.22 Cost Estimating Worksheet: ISO 26262

467. What can be included?

468. What is the estimated labor cost today based upon this information?

469. How will the results be shared and to whom?

470. Identify the timeframe necessary to monitor progress and collect data to determine how the selected measure has changed?

471. Does the ISO 26262 project provide innovative ways for stakeholders to overcome obstacles or deliver better outcomes?

472. What happens to any remaining funds not used?

473. Is it feasible to establish a control group arrangement?

474. What is the purpose of estimating?

475. Is the ISO 26262 project responsive to community need?

476. What additional ISO 26262 project(s) could be initiated as a result of this ISO 26262 project?

477. What costs are to be estimated?

478. Ask: are others positioned to know, are others credible, and will others cooperate?

479. Will the ISO 26262 project collaborate with the local community and leverage resources?

480. Who is best positioned to know and assist in identifying corresponding factors?

481. What will others want?

482. Can a trend be established from historical performance data on the selected measure and are the criteria for using trend analysis or forecasting methods met?

2.23 Cost Baseline: ISO 26262

483. At which frequency ?

484. On budget?

485. Should a more thorough impact analysis be conducted?

486. Have all the product or service deliverables been accepted by the customer?

487. What threats might prevent you from getting there?

488. What do you want to measure ?

489. What is it ?

490. How likely is it to go wrong?

491. Eac -estimate at completion, what is the total job expected to cost?

492. How accurate do cost estimates need to be?

493. What is the most important thing to do next to make your ISO 26262 project successful?

494. Escalation criteria met?

495. Does the suggested change request seem to represent a necessary enhancement to the product?

496. Have all approved changes to the schedule baseline been identified and impact on the ISO 26262 project documented?

497. How difficult will it be to do specific tasks on the ISO 26262 project?

498. Have the lessons learned been filed with the ISO 26262 project Management Office?

499. What does a good WBS NOT look like?

2.24 Quality Management Plan: ISO 26262

500. How does your organization ensure the reliability, accuracy, timeliness, security and accessibility of data and information?

501. Is there a Quality Management Plan?

502. How do senior leaders create your organizational focus on customers and other stakeholders?

503. Do you keep back-up copies of any data?

504. Have all necessary approvals been obtained?

505. How are calibration records kept?

506. Who else should be involved ?

507. How do you check in-coming sample material?

508. How does your organization use comparative data and information to improve organizational performance?

509. How does your organization make it easy for customers to seek assistance or complain?

510. How do you ensure that your sampling methods and procedures meet your data quality objectives?

511. Who is responsible?

512. Are you meeting the quality standards?

513. Does the program use modeling in the permitting or decision-making processes?

514. Are there trends or hot spots?

515. Sampling part of task?

516. What process do you use to minimize errors, defects, and rework?

517. What are your organizations key processes (product, service, business, and support)?

518. Can it be done better?

519. How do your action plans support the strategic objectives?

2.25 Quality Metrics: ISO 26262

520. Is material complete (and does it meet the standards)?

521. How exactly do you define when differences exist?

522. Subjective quality component: customer satisfaction, how do you measure it?

523. What about still open problems?

524. What method of measurement do you use?

525. Is the reporting frequency appropriate?

526. How do you calculate corresponding metrics?

527. Was review conducted per standard protocols?

528. What metrics do you measure?

529. Were quality attributes reported?

530. Is quality culture a competitive advantage?

531. Is a risk containment plan in place?

532. Was material distributed on time?

533. When is the security analysis testing complete?

534. What if the biggest risk to your business were the

already stated people who do not complain?

535. How do you communicate results and findings to upper management?

536. Do you know how much profit a 10% decrease in waste would generate?

537. Do you stratify metrics by product or site?

538. Should a modifier be included?

2.26 Process Improvement Plan: ISO 26262

539. Does your process ensure quality?

540. Where do you focus?

541. What is quality and how will you ensure it?

542. What personnel are the change agents for your initiative?

543. Where do you want to be?

544. Have the supporting tools been developed or acquired?

545. How do you manage quality?

546. What personnel are the coaches for your initiative?

547. Has the time line required to move measurement results from the points of collection to databases or users been established?

548. Why quality management?

549. What is the return on investment?

550. The motive is determined by asking, Why do you want to achieve this goal?

551. Have the frequency of collection and the points in the process where measurements will be made been determined?

552. Has a process guide to collect the data been developed?

553. Are you making progress on your improvement plan?

554. Are you making progress on the improvement framework?

555. What lessons have you learned so far?

556. Modeling current processes is great, and will you ever see a return on that investment?

2.27 Responsibility Assignment Matrix: ISO 26262

557. Does the contractors system provide unit or lot costs when applicable?

558. Competencies and craftsmanship – what competencies are necessary and what level?

559. Are detailed work packages planned as far in advance as practicable?

560. Are all elements of indirect expense identified to overhead cost budgets of ISO 26262 projections?

561. Does a missing responsibility indicate that the current ISO 26262 project is not yet fully understood?

562. Detailed schedules which support control account and work package start and completion dates/events?

563. How many hours by each staff member/rate?

564. Does the scheduling system identify in a timely manner the status of work?

565. Are records maintained to show how undistributed budgets are controlled?

566. ISO 26262 projected economic escalation?

567. Are people encouraged to bring up issues?

568. Are the requirements for all items of overhead established by rational, traceable processes?

569. Past experience – the person or the group worked at something similar in the past?

570. Is cost and schedule performance measurement done in a consistent, systematic manner?

571. What is the business need?

572. Are significant decision points, constraints, and interfaces identified as key milestones?

573. Time-phased control account budgets?

574. Major functional areas of contract effort?

2.28 Roles and Responsibilities: ISO 26262

575. Is the data complete?

576. Is there a training program in place for stakeholders covering expectations, roles and responsibilities and any addition knowledge others need to be good stakeholders?

577. Attainable / achievable: the goal is attainable; can you actually accomplish the goal?

578. What should you highlight for improvement?

579. What should you do now to prepare yourself for a promotion, increased responsibilities or a different job?

580. Does the team have access to and ability to use data analysis tools?

581. Are ISO 26262 project team roles and responsibilities identified and documented?

582. What expectations were met?

583. Was the expectation clearly communicated?

584. Concern: where are you limited or have no authority, where you can not influence?

585. What expectations were NOT met?

586. Once the responsibilities are defined for the ISO 26262 project, have the deliverables, roles and responsibilities been clearly communicated to every participant?

587. Be specific; avoid generalities. Thank you and great work alone are insufficient. What exactly do you appreciate and why?

588. Are ISO 26262 project team roles and responsibilities identified and documented?

589. Authority: what areas/ISO 26262 projects in your work do you have the authority to decide upon and act on the already stated decisions?

590. Are the quality assurance functions and related roles and responsibilities clearly defined?

591. Do the values and practices inherent in the culture of your organization foster or hinder the process?

592. What specific behaviors did you observe?

2.29 Human Resource Management Plan: ISO 26262

593. Was your organizations estimating methodology being used and followed?

594. Are key risk mitigation strategies added to the ISO 26262 project schedule?

595. Is your organization primarily focused on a specific industry?

596. Has the ISO 26262 project manager been identified?

597. Are issues raised, assessed, actioned, and resolved in a timely and efficient manner?

598. Has the ISO 26262 project scope been baselined?

599. Do people have the competencies to meet the strategic objectives?

600. Is ISO 26262 project status reviewed with the steering and executive teams at appropriate intervals?

601. Are governance roles and responsibilities documented?

602. Responsiveness to change and the resulting demands for different skills and abilities?

603. Have ISO 26262 project success criteria been

defined?

604. Have all involved ISO 26262 project stakeholders and work groups committed to the ISO 26262 project?

605. Is the ISO 26262 project schedule available for all ISO 26262 project team members to review?

606. Is there an on-going process in place to monitor ISO 26262 project risks?

607. Were escalated issues resolved promptly?

608. Has the schedule been baselined?

2.30 Communications Management Plan: ISO 26262

609. Do you ask; can you recommend others for you to talk with about this initiative?

610. How will the person responsible for executing the communication item be notified?

611. How were corresponding initiatives successful?

612. What communications method?

613. In your work, how much time is spent on stakeholder identification?

614. Do you prepare stakeholder engagement plans?

615. Who is involved as you identify stakeholders?

616. Who needs to know and how much?

617. Do you have members of your team responsible for certain stakeholders?

618. What is the stakeholders level of authority?

619. Are stakeholders internal or external?

620. Are there potential barriers between the team and the stakeholder?

621. Which stakeholders are thought leaders,

influences, or early adopters?

622. Who have you worked with in past, similar initiatives?

623. Are others part of the communications management plan?

624. Will messages be directly related to the release strategy or phases of the ISO 26262 project?

625. How often do you engage with stakeholders?

626. Conflict resolution -which method when?

627. What approaches to you feel are the best ones to use?

628. Why manage stakeholders?

2.31 Risk Management Plan: ISO 26262

629. Is the customer technically sophisticated in the product area?

630. What risks are necessary to achieve success?

631. Are you on schedule?

632. Where are you confronted with risks during the business phases?

633. How well were you able to manage your risk before?

634. Do benefits and chances of success outweigh potential damage if success is not attained?

635. Does the ISO 26262 project have the authority and ability to avoid the risk?

636. Costs associated with late delivery or a defective product?

637. Market risk -will the new service or product be useful to your organization or marketable to others?

638. Is there additional information that would make you more confident about your analysis?

639. Have top software and customer managers formally committed to support the ISO 26262 project?

640. Are testing tools available and suitable?

641. Degree of confidence in estimated size estimate?

642. How are risk analvsis and prioritization performed?

643. For software; are compilers and code generators available and suitable for the product to be built?

644. Maximize short-term return on investment?

645. What can go wrong?

646. What are the chances the risk event will occur?

647. Are ISO 26262 project requirements stable?

2.32 Risk Register: ISO 26262

648. What can be done about it?

649. Which key risks have ineffective responses or outstanding improvement actions?

650. Risk categories: what are the main categories of risks that should be addressed on this ISO 26262 project?

651. What is a Community Risk Register?

652. Can the likelihood and impact of failing to achieve corresponding recommendations and action plans be assessed?

653. Are implemented controls working as others should?

654. Schedule impact/severity estimated range (workdays) assume the event happens, what is the potential impact?

655. What are the assumptions and current status that support the assessment of the risk?

656. What is a Risk?

657. How are risks graded?

658. What may happen or not go according to plan?

659. What are the major risks facing the ISO 26262

project?

660. Severity Prediction?

661. How well are risks controlled?

662. What should the audit role be in establishing a risk management process?

663. What evidence do you have to justify the likelihood score of the risk (audit, incident report, claim, complaints, inspection, internal review)?

664. Do you require further engagement?

665. Preventative actions - planned actions to reduce the likelihood a risk will occur and/or reduce the seriousness should it occur. What should you do now?

666. What are you going to do to limit the ISO 26262 projects risk exposure due to the identified risks?

2.33 Probability and Impact Assessment: ISO 26262

667. How are you working with risks?

668. How would you suggest monitoring for risk transition indicators?

669. Risk data quality assessment - what is the quality of the data used to determine or assess the risk?

670. Monitoring of the overall ISO 26262 project status – are there any changes in the ISO 26262 project that can effect and cause new possible risks?

671. Mitigation -how can you avoid the risk?

672. How is risk handled within this ISO 26262 project organization?

673. Risk categorization -which of your categories has more risk than others?

674. Have decisions that should be left open because of inadequate information on technology been identified and responsibility assigned for reducing the uncertainty?

675. Are requirements fully understood by the software engineering team and customers?

676. Do you train all developers in the process?

677. Have you ascribed a level of confidence to every critical technical objective?

678. Who will be responsible for a slippage?

679. How carefully have the potential competitors been identified?

680. What are the current demands of the customer?

681. What are the channels available for distribution to the customer?

682. What are the tools and techniques used in managing the challenges faced?

683. What is the level of experience available with your organization?

684. What is the experience (performance, attitude, business ethics, etc.) in the past with contractors?

685. How would you assess the risk management process in the ISO 26262 project?

686. Is the customer willing to commit significant time to the requirements gathering process?

2.34 Probability and Impact Matrix: ISO 26262

687. How are risks and risk management perceived in the ISO 26262 project?

688. How much risk do others need to take?

689. What are the preparations required for facing difficulties?

690. Is the delay in one subISO 26262 project going to affect another?

691. How do you define a risk?

692. What are ways to measure and evaluate risks?

693. Do you use any methods to analyze risks?

694. Does the customer have a solid idea of what is required?

695. Who should be notified of the occurrence of each of the risk indicators?

696. Mandated specific features?

697. How completely has the customer been identified?

698. Do the people have the right combinations of skills?

699. Will there be an increase in the political conservatism?

700. What action would you take to the identified risks in the ISO 26262 project?

701. Mandated delivery date?

702. Are the best people available?

703. Amount of reused software?

704. What risks were tracked?

705. Are the risk data complete?

2.35 Risk Data Sheet: ISO 26262

706. What is the likelihood of it happening?

707. What were the Causes that contributed?

708. How can hazards be reduced?

709. What if client refuses?

710. Is the data sufficiently specified in terms of the type of failure being analyzed, and its frequency or probability?

711. What are the main threats to your existence?

712. What can happen?

713. What are you here for (Mission)?

714. What can you do?

715. How do you handle product safely?

716. What actions can be taken to eliminate or remove risk?

717. Risk of what?

718. Who has a vested interest in how you perform as your organization (our stakeholders)?

719. What will be the consequences if it happens?

720. What are you trying to achieve (Objectives)?

721. What are you weak at and therefore need to do better?

722. Potential for recurrence?

723. Whom do you serve (customers)?

724. Has the most cost-effective solution been chosen?

2.36 Procurement Management Plan: ISO 26262

725. Are adequate resources provided for the quality assurance function?

726. What are your quality assurance overheads?

727. Has a provision been made to reassess ISO 26262 project risks at various ISO 26262 project stages?

728. Are ISO 26262 project leaders committed to this ISO 26262 project full time?

729. Are the ISO 26262 project team members located locally to the users/stakeholders?

730. Are post milestone ISO 26262 project reviews (PMPR) conducted with your organization at least once a year?

731. Are metrics used to evaluate and manage Vendors?

732. Is there a requirements change management processes in place?

733. Have lessons learned been conducted after each ISO 26262 project release?

734. What types of contracts will be used?

735. Are vendor invoices audited for accuracy before

payment?

736. Are status reports received per the ISO 26262 project Plan?

737. Has the ISO 26262 project manager been identified?

738. How and when do you enter into ISO 26262 project Procurement Management?

739. Are assumptions being identified, recorded, analyzed, qualified and closed?

740. Is there an onboarding process in place?

2.37 Source Selection Criteria: ISO 26262

741. What can not be disclosed?

742. How do you encourage efficiency and consistency?

743. What are the most common types of rating systems?

744. How can the methods of publicizing the buy be tailored to yield more effective price competition?

745. How is past performance evaluated?

746. Is experience evaluated?

747. What is the role of counsel in the procurement process?

748. Do proposed hours support content and schedule?

749. Can you reasonably estimate total organization requirements for the coming year?

750. How much past performance information should be requested?

751. Does an evaluation need to include the identification of strengths and weaknesses?

752. What is the basis of an estimate and what assumptions were made?

753. What past performance information should be requested?

754. Does the evaluation of any change include an impact analysis; how will the change affect the scope, time, cost, and quality of the goods or services being provided?

755. What instructions should be provided regarding oral presentations?

756. What procedures are followed when a contractor requires access to classified information or a significant quantity of special material/information?

757. What should be considered?

758. What information is to be provided and when should it be provided?

759. What common questions or problems are associated with debriefings?

760. When is it appropriate to issue a Draft Request for Proposal (DRFP)?

2.38 Stakeholder Management Plan: ISO 26262

761. Where does the information come from?

762. Are there standards for code development?

763. How, to whom and how frequently will Risk status be reported?

764. Which impacts could serve as impediments?

765. Have ISO 26262 project success criteria been defined?

766. Are there checklists created to demine if all quality processes are followed?

767. Is there general agreement & acceptance of the current status and progress of the ISO 26262 project?

768. Are communication systems currently in place appropriate?

769. Were ISO 26262 project team members involved in the development of activity & task decomposition?

770. Why would you develop a ISO 26262 project Business Plan?

771. Are all payments made according to the contract(s)?

772. Have all documents been archived in a ISO 26262 project repository for each release?

773. Are updated ISO 26262 project time & resource estimates reasonable based on the current ISO 26262 project stage?

774. Have the key elements of a coherent ISO 26262 project management strategy been established?

2.39 Change Management Plan: ISO 26262

775. Are there any restrictions on who can receive the communications?

776. What tasks are needed?

777. Has the training co-ordinator been provided with the training details and put in place the necessary arrangements?

778. Has the target training audience been identified and nominated?

779. What processes are in place to manage knowledge about the ISO 26262 project?

780. When does it make sense to customize?

781. What are the specific target groups/audiences that will be impacted by this change?

782. What is the most positive interpretation it can receive?

783. Where will the funds come from?

784. Do you need new systems?

785. Impact of systems implementation on organization change?

786. Is there an adequate supply of people for the new roles?

787. Are there resource implications for your communications strategy?

788. Change invariability confront many relationships especially the already stated that require a set of behaviours What roles with in your organization are affected and how?

789. How will the stakeholders share information and transfer knowledge?

790. How much ISO 26262 project management is needed?

791. When to start change management?

792. What is the most cynical response it can receive?

793. What is the reason for the communication?

3.0 Executing Process Group: ISO 26262

794. Is the ISO 26262 project making progress in helping to achieve the set results?

795. What is in place for ensuring adequate change control on ISO 26262 projects that involve outside contracts?

796. What are the main parts of the scope statement?

797. What business situation is being addressed?

798. What are the main processes included in ISO 26262 project quality management?

799. How could you control progress of your ISO 26262 project?

800. Who will be the main sponsor?

801. What are the critical steps involved in selecting measures and initiatives?

802. When is the appropriate time to bring the scorecard to Board meetings?

803. Do the partners have sufficient financial capacity to keep up the benefits produced by the programme?

804. What is involved in the solicitation process?

805. If action is called for, what form should it take?

806. How does the job market and current state of the economy affect human resource management?

807. After how many days will the lease cost be the same as the purchase cost for the equipment?

808. In what way has the program come up with innovative measures for problem-solving?

809. How is ISO 26262 project performance information created and distributed?

810. What does it mean to take a systems view of a ISO 26262 project?

811. What is the shortest possible time it will take to complete this ISO 26262 project?

812. What are deliverables of your ISO 26262 project?

3.1 Team Member Status Report: ISO 26262

813. How does this product, good, or service meet the needs of the ISO 26262 project and your organization as a whole?

814. Do you have an Enterprise ISO 26262 project Management Office (EPMO)?

815. Are the products of your organizations ISO 26262 projects meeting customers objectives?

816. Is there evidence that staff is taking a more professional approach toward management of your organizations ISO 26262 projects?

817. Does your organization have the means (staff, money, contract, etc.) to produce or to acquire the product, good, or service?

818. How can you make it practical?

819. Are the attitudes of staff regarding ISO 26262 project work improving?

820. Does every department have to have a ISO 26262 project Manager on staff?

821. How it is to be done?

822. How will resource planning be done?

823. Does the product, good, or service already exist within your organization?

824. Will the staff do training or is that done by a third party?

825. When a teams productivity and success depend on collaboration and the efficient flow of information, what generally fails them?

826. What specific interest groups do you have in place?

827. Why is it to be done?

828. How much risk is involved?

829. The problem with Reward & Recognition Programs is that the truly deserving people all too often get left out. How can you make it practical?

830. Are your organizations ISO 26262 projects more successful over time?

831. What is to be done?

3.2 Change Request: ISO 26262

832. Will there be a change request form in use?

833. How many times must the change be modified or presented to the change control board before it is approved?

834. What must be taken into consideration when introducing change control programs?

835. Will this change conflict with other requirements changes (e.g., lead to conflicting operational scenarios)?

836. What is a Change Request Form?

837. Which requirements attributes affect the risk to reliability the most?

838. How can you ensure that changes have been made properly?

839. Who will perform the change?

840. What are the requirements for urgent changes?

841. Have all related configuration items been properly updated?

842. Who can suggest changes?

843. Who is responsible to authorize changes?

844. Why were your requested changes rejected or not made?

845. How are changes requested (forms, method of communication)?

846. Has the change been highlighted and documented in the CSCI?

847. Who needs to approve change requests?

848. What kind of information about the change request needs to be captured?

849. Will all change requests be unconditionally tracked through this process?

850. Who is included in the change control team?

3.3 Change Log: ISO 26262

851. Is the change request open, closed or pending?

852. Where do changes come from?

853. Is this a mandatory replacement?

854. Is the change request within ISO 26262 project scope?

855. How does this change affect the timeline of the schedule?

856. Is the requested change request a result of changes in other ISO 26262 project(s)?

857. How does this change affect scope?

858. Is the change backward compatible without limitations?

859. When was the request submitted?

860. Do the described changes impact on the integrity or security of the system?

861. How does this relate to the standards developed for specific business processes?

862. Is the submitted change a new change or a modification of a previously approved change?

863. Who initiated the change request?

864. When was the request approved?

865. Will the ISO 26262 project fail if the change request is not executed?

866. Does the suggested change request represent a desired enhancement to the products functionality?

3.4 Decision Log: ISO 26262

867. With whom was the decision shared or considered?

868. What alternatives/risks were considered?

869. How does the use a Decision Support System influence the strategies/tactics or costs?

870. Who will be given a copy of this document and where will it be kept?

871. How does an increasing emphasis on cost containment influence the strategies and tactics used?

872. Meeting purpose; why does this team meet?

873. Is your opponent open to a non-traditional workflow, or will it likely challenge anything you do?

874. Do strategies and tactics aimed at less than full control reduce the costs of management or simply shift the cost burden?

875. How consolidated and comprehensive a story can you tell by capturing currently available incident data in a central location and through a log of key decisions during an incident?

876. It becomes critical to track and periodically revisit both operational effectiveness; Are you noticing all that you need to, and are you interpreting what you

see effectively?

877. How do you know when you are achieving it?

878. What is the average size of your matters in an applicable measurement?

879. How effective is maintaining the log at facilitating organizational learning?

880. What eDiscovery problem or issue did your organization set out to fix or make better?

881. Which variables make a critical difference?

882. Linked to original objective?

883. What are the cost implications?

884. Does anything need to be adjusted?

885. Decision-making process; how will the team make decisions?

886. At what point in time does loss become unacceptable?

3.5 Quality Audit: ISO 26262

887. Does everyone know what they are supposed to be doing, how and why?

888. How does your organization know that the range and quality of its social and recreational services and facilities are appropriately effective and constructive in meeting the needs of staff?

889. How does your organization know that its quality of teaching is appropriately effective and constructive?

890. Have personnel cleanliness and health requirements been established?

891. Is there any content that may be legally actionable?

892. How does your organization know that it provides a safe and healthy environment?

893. Health and safety arrangements; stress management workshops. How does your organization know that it provides a safe and healthy environment?

894. How does your organization know that the research supervision provided to its staff is appropriately effective and constructive?

895. How does your organization know that its system for supporting staff research capability is appropriately effective and constructive?

896. Are complaint files maintained?

897. What are the main things that hinder your ability to do a good job?

898. How does your organization know that its system for ensuring a positive organizational climate is appropriately effective and constructive?

899. Is quality audit a prerequisite for program accreditation or program recognition?

900. How does your organization know that its management of its ethical responsibilities is appropriately effective and constructive?

901. How does your organization know that its system for recruiting the best staff possible are appropriately effective and constructive?

902. What does an analysis of your organizations staff profile suggest in terms of its planning, and how is this being addressed?

903. How does your organization know that its system for managing intellectual property issues is appropriately effective, constructive and fair?

904. How does your organization know that its planning processes are appropriately effective and constructive?

905. Are training programs documented?

906. How does your organization know that its

relationship with its (past) staff is appropriately effective and constructive?

3.6 Team Directory: ISO 26262

907. Process decisions: do job conditions warrant additional actions to collect job information and document on-site activity?

908. Process decisions: are contractors adequately prosecuting the work?

909. Decisions: is the most suitable form of contract being used?

910. Who will write the meeting minutes and distribute?

911. When will you produce deliverables?

912. Does a ISO 26262 project team directory list all resources assigned to the ISO 26262 project?

913. Process decisions: are there any statutory or regulatory issues relevant to the timely execution of work?

914. What are you going to deliver or accomplish?

915. How does the team resolve conflicts and ensure tasks are completed?

916. Days from the time the issue is identified?

917. Process decisions: which organizational elements and which individuals will be assigned management functions?

918. Decisions: what could be done better to improve the quality of the constructed product?

919. Do purchase specifications and configurations match requirements?

920. Have you decided when to celebrate the ISO 26262 projects completion date?

921. How will you accomplish and manage the objectives?

922. Who will report ISO 26262 project status to all stakeholders?

923. Who should receive information (all stakeholders)?

924. Process decisions: how well was task order work performed?

925. When does information need to be distributed?

3.7 Team Operating Agreement: ISO 26262

926. Must your team members rely on the expertise of other members to complete tasks?

927. Must your members collaborate successfully to complete ISO 26262 projects?

928. Do you call or email participants to ensure understanding, follow-through and commitment to the meeting outcomes?

929. How will you resolve conflict efficiently and respectfully?

930. Methodologies: how will key team processes be implemented, such as training, research, work deliverable production, review and approval processes, knowledge management, and meeting procedures?

931. Are there more than two functional areas represented by your team?

932. Why does your organization want to participate in teaming?

933. The method to be used in the decision making process; Will it be consensus, majority rule, or the supervisor having the final say?

934. Are there the right people on your team?

935. What went well?

936. Do you ensure that all participants know how to use the required technology?

937. Do you determine the meeting length and time of day?

938. Communication protocols: how will the team communicate?

939. Do you prevent individuals from dominating the meeting?

940. What administrative supports will be put in place to support the team and the teams supervisor?

941. How will you divide work equitably?

942. Do you solicit member feedback about meetings and what would make them better?

943. Do team members need to frequently communicate as a full group to make timely decisions?

944. Did you prepare participants for the next meeting?

945. To whom do you deliver your services?

3.8 Team Performance Assessment: ISO 26262

946. To what degree are the relative importance and priority of the goals clear to all team members?

947. To what degree are fresh input and perspectives systematically caught and added (for example, through information and analysis, new members, and senior sponsors)?

948. Effects of crew composition on crew performance: Does the whole equal the sum of its parts?

949. To what degree can team members frequently and easily communicate with one another?

950. To what degree will the approach capitalize on and enhance the skills of all team members in a manner that takes into consideration other demands on members of the team?

951. To what degree can team members meet frequently enough to accomplish the teams ends?

952. When a reviewer complains about method variance, what is the essence of the complaint?

953. To what degree do team members agree with the goals, relative importance, and the ways in which achievement will be measured?

954. How do you encourage members to learn from each other?

955. Can team performance be reliably measured in simulator and live exercises using the same assessment tool?

956. To what degree will the team ensure that all members equitably share the work essential to the success of the team?

957. To what degree are the goals realistic?

958. To what degree are sub-teams possible or necessary?

959. To what degree do team members articulate the teams work approach?

960. To what degree does the teams approach to its work allow for modification and improvement over time?

961. To what degree are staff involved as partners in the improvement process?

962. To what degree will the team adopt a concrete, clearly understood, and agreed-upon approach that will result in achievement of the teams goals?

963. To what degree is the team cognizant of small wins to be celebrated along the way?

964. To what degree are corresponding categories of skills either actually or potentially represented across the membership?

965. If you are worried about method variance before you collect data, what sort of design elements might you include to reduce or eliminate the threat of method variance?

3.9 Team Member Performance Assessment: ISO 26262

966. What steps have you taken to improve performance?

967. What is a significant fact or event?

968. Does the rater (supervisor) have the authority or responsibility to tell an employee that the employees performance is unsatisfactory?

969. What, if any, steps are available for employees who feel they have been unfairly or inaccurately rated?

970. What makes them effective?

971. What is the Business Management Oversight Process?

972. How do you determine which data are the most important to use, analyze, or review?

973. What innovations (if any) are developed to realize goals?

974. To what degree do team members frequently explore the teams purpose and its implications?

975. What resources do you need?

976. How should adaptive assessments be

implemented?

977. To what degree does the team possess adequate membership to achieve its ends?

978. Goals met?

979. What qualities does a successful Team leader possess?

980. How does your team work together?

981. What are they responsible for?

982. How do you start collaborating?

983. What are top priorities?

984. To what degree are the skill areas critical to team performance present?

3.10 Issue Log: ISO 26262

985. Are there too many who have an interest in some aspect of your work?

986. What approaches do you use?

987. What is the status of the issue?

988. Who do you turn to if you have questions?

989. Is the issue log kept in a safe place?

990. In classifying stakeholders, which approach to do so are you using?

991. Are the stakeholders getting the information they need, are they consulted, are concerns addressed?

992. Which team member will work with each stakeholder?

993. How do you manage human resources?

994. How do you manage communications?

995. Which stakeholders can influence others?

996. Why do you manage human resources?

997. Do you often overlook a key stakeholder or stakeholder group?

998. What does the stakeholder need from the team?

999. Are they needed?

1000. How much time does it take to do it?

4.0 Monitoring and Controlling Process Group: ISO 26262

1001. Did the ISO 26262 project team have the right skills?

1002. How well defined and documented were the ISO 26262 project management processes you chose to use?

1003. Feasibility: how much money, time, and effort can you put into this?

1004. How will staff learn how to use the deliverables?

1005. Purpose: toward what end is the evaluation being conducted?

1006. User: who wants the information and what are they interested in?

1007. How is agile portfolio management done?

1008. What resources (both financial and non-financial) are available/needed?

1009. Who needs to be involved in the planning?

1010. How was the program set-up initiated?

1011. Key stakeholders to work with. How many potential communications channels exist on the ISO 26262 project?

1012. Where is the Risk in the ISO 26262 project?

1013. Where is the Risk in the ISO 26262 project?

1014. Just how important is your work to the overall success of the ISO 26262 project?

1015. How well did the chosen processes fit the needs of the ISO 26262 project?

1016. How many potential communications channels exist on the ISO 26262 project?

4.1 Project Performance Report: ISO 26262

1017. To what degree do all members feel responsible for all agreed-upon measures?

1018. To what degree do team members feel that the purpose of the team is important, if not exciting?

1019. To what degree can all members engage in open and interactive considerations?

1020. To what degree are the demands of the task compatible with and converge with the mission and functions of the formal organization?

1021. To what degree does the teams purpose contain themes that are particularly meaningful and memorable?

1022. To what degree are the structures of the formal organization consistent with the behaviors in the informal organization?

1023. What degree are the relative importance and priority of the goals clear to all team members?

1024. To what degree do the structures of the formal organization motivate taskrelevant behavior and facilitate task completion?

1025. To what degree do team members understand one anothers roles and skills?

1026. How will procurement be coordinated with other ISO 26262 project aspects, such as scheduling and performance reporting?

1027. To what degree can the team measure progress against specific goals?

1028. Next Steps?

1029. To what degree does the teams work approach provide opportunity for members to engage in results-based evaluation?

1030. To what degree can the cognitive capacity of individuals accommodate the flow of information?

1031. To what degree does the teams work approach provide opportunity for members to engage in open interaction?

1032. To what degree is there a sense that only the team can succeed?

4.2 Variance Analysis: ISO 26262

1033. Are management actions taken to reduce indirect costs when there are significant adverse variances?

1034. What is the total budget for the ISO 26262 project (including estimates for authorized and unpriced work)?

1035. Are procedures for variance analysis documented and consistently applied at the control account level and selected WBS and organizational levels at least monthly as a routine task?

1036. Are records maintained to show how management reserves are used?

1037. Are material costs reported within the same period as that in which BCWP is earned for that material?

1038. How do you evaluate the impact of schedule changes, work around, et?

1039. What can be the cause of an increase in costs?

1040. Are the bases and rates for allocating costs from each indirect pool consistently applied?

1041. What is the performance to date and material commitment?

1042. Is there a logical explanation for any variance?

1043. Did a new competitor enter the market?

1044. Are the wbs and organizational levels for application of the ISO 26262 projected overhead costs identified?

1045. Can process improvements lead to unfavorable variances?

1046. What does a favorable labor efficiency variance mean?

1047. Does the contractors system include procedures for measuring the performance of critical subcontractors?

1048. What business event caused the fluctuation?

1049. Do work packages consist of discrete tasks which are adequately described?

1050. What is exceptional?

4.3 Earned Value Status: ISO 26262

1051. How much is it going to cost by the finish?

1052. Are you hitting your ISO 26262 projects targets?

1053. If earned value management (EVM) is so good in determining the true status of a ISO 26262 project and ISO 26262 project its completion, why is it that hardly any one uses it in information systems related ISO 26262 projects?

1054. When is it going to finish?

1055. Earned value can be used in almost any ISO 26262 project situation and in almost any ISO 26262 project environment. it may be used on large ISO 26262 projects, medium sized ISO 26262 projects, tiny ISO 26262 projects (in cut-down form), complex and simple ISO 26262 projects and in any market sector. some people, of course, know all about earned value, they have used it for years - but perhaps not as effectively as they could have?

1056. Where are your problem areas?

1057. Validation is a process of ensuring that the developed system will actually achieve the stakeholders desired outcomes; Are you building the right product? What do you validate?

1058. Verification is a process of ensuring that the developed system satisfies the stakeholders agreements and specifications; Are you building the product right? What do you verify?

1059. Where is evidence-based earned value in your organization reported?

1060. What is the unit of forecast value?

1061. How does this compare with other ISO 26262 projects?

4.4 Risk Audit: ISO 26262

1062. Are there any forms the staff is required to sign?

1063. Number of users of the product?

1064. Are corresponding safety and risk management policies posted for all to see?

1065. What can be measured?

1066. Is the customer willing to establish rapid communication links with the developer?

1067. Do you have a procedure for dealing with complaints?

1068. Should additional substantive testing be conducted because of the risk audit results?

1069. What are the risks that could stop you from achieving your objectives?

1070. What can you do to manage outcomes?

1071. Do you have written and signed agreements/contracts in place for each paid staff member?

1072. Do you have financial policies and procedures in place to guide officers of your organization/treasurer/general members?

1073. Is ISO 26262 project scope stable?

1074. What are the differences and similarities between strategic and operational risks in your organization?

1075. What is the anticipated volatility of the requirements?

1076. Are risk management strategies documented?

1077. Tradeoff: how much risk can be tolerated and still deliver the products where they need to be?

1078. The halo effect in business risk audits: can strategic risk assessment bias auditor judgment about accounting details?

1079. Have you reviewed your constitution within the last twelve months?

1080. Do end-users have realistic expectations?

4.5 Contractor Status Report: ISO 26262

1081. What is the average response time for answering a support call?

1082. How is risk transferred?

1083. What was the actual budget or estimated cost for your organizations services?

1084. If applicable; describe your standard schedule for new software version releases. Are new software version releases included in the standard maintenance plan?

1085. Who can list a ISO 26262 project as organization experience, your organization or a previous employee of your organization?

1086. What process manages the contracts?

1087. How long have you been using the services?

1088. What was the overall budget or estimated cost?

1089. What was the final actual cost?

1090. What are the minimum and optimal bandwidth requirements for the proposed solution?

1091. Are there contractual transfer concerns?

1092. Describe how often regular updates are made to the proposed solution. Are corresponding regular updates included in the standard maintenance plan?

1093. What was the budget or estimated cost for your organizations services?

1094. How does the proposed individual meet each requirement?

4.6 Formal Acceptance: ISO 26262

1095. Is formal acceptance of the ISO 26262 project product documented and distributed?

1096. Who would use it?

1097. Was the ISO 26262 project goal achieved?

1098. Was the client satisfied with the ISO 26262 project results?

1099. Do you buy-in installation services?

1100. What can you do better next time?

1101. Have all comments been addressed?

1102. Was business value realized?

1103. Do you perform formal acceptance or burn-in tests?

1104. Does it do what client said it would?

1105. Did the ISO 26262 project manager and team act in a professional and ethical manner?

1106. What lessons were learned about your ISO 26262 project management methodology?

1107. How does your team plan to obtain formal acceptance on your ISO 26262 project?

1108. General estimate of the costs and times to complete the ISO 26262 project?

1109. Was the ISO 26262 project managed well?

1110. What was done right?

1111. What is the Acceptance Management Process?

1112. Was the ISO 26262 project work done on time, within budget, and according to specification?

1113. How well did the team follow the methodology?

1114. Did the ISO 26262 project achieve its MOV?

5.0 Closing Process Group: ISO 26262

1115. How well did the team follow the chosen processes?

1116. What is the risk of failure to your organization?

1117. Is this an updated ISO 26262 project Proposal Document?

1118. What could have been improved?

1119. Did you do things well?

1120. What were the desired outcomes?

1121. Was the user/client satisfied with the end product?

1122. What do you need to do?

1123. What level of risk does the proposed budget represent to the ISO 26262 project?

1124. Were the outcomes different from the already stated planned?

1125. Did the ISO 26262 project team have enough people to execute the ISO 26262 project plan?

1126. Did the delivered product meet the specified requirements and goals of the ISO 26262 project?

1127. Were cost budgets met?

1128. What areas does the group agree are the biggest success on the ISO 26262 project?

1129. What areas were overlooked on this ISO 26262 project?

1130. What was learned?

5.1 Procurement Audit: ISO 26262

1131. Were there no inconsistencies between the several tender documents?

1132. Are buyers prohibited from accepting gifts from vendors?

1133. Has it been determined how large a portion of the procurement portfolio should be managed by the procurement function/unit and how large a portion that should be managed locally?

1134. Are the rules for automatic payment in computer programs approved by management prior to implementation?

1135. Are all purchase orders reviewed by someone other than the individual preparing the purchase order (reasonableness of order and vendor selection)?

1136. Are there regular accounting reconciliations of contract payments, transactions and inventory?

1137. Did the conditions included in the contract protect the risk of non-performance by the supplier and were there no conflicting provisions?

1138. Have late payment interests been rewarded and could they have been avoided?

1139. Were the documents received scrutinised for completion and adherence to stated conditions before the tenders were evaluated?

1140. Could the bidders assess the economic risks the successful bidder would be responsible for, thus limiting the inclusion of extra charges for risk?

1141. Are advantages and disadvantages of in house production, outsourcing and Public Private Partnerships considered?

1142. Have guidelines been set up for how the procurement process should be conducted?

1143. Are unusual uses of organization funds investigated?

1144. Are cases of double payment duly prevented and corrected?

1145. Is there no evidence of any external or superior pressure to reach a specific result?

1146. Was timely and equal access to contract documents and information provided to all candidates?

1147. Is the performance of the procurement function/unit benchmarked with other procurement functions/units in the different stages of the procurement process?

1148. Are approval limits definitive as to amount and classification of expenditure?

1149. Are there performance targets on value for money obtained and cost savings?

1150. Did the conditions of contract comply with the detail provided in the procurement documents and with the outcome of the procurement procedure followed?

5.2 Contract Close-Out: ISO 26262

1151. Have all acceptance criteria been met prior to final payment to contractors?

1152. What happens to the recipient of services?

1153. Parties: who is involved?

1154. How is the contracting office notified of the automatic contract close-out?

1155. Have all contracts been completed?

1156. Change in circumstances?

1157. Was the contract type appropriate?

1158. What is capture management?

1159. How/when used ?

1160. Was the contract complete without requiring numerous changes and revisions?

1161. Was the contract sufficiently clear so as not to result in numerous disputes and misunderstandings?

1162. Are the signers the authorized officials?

1163. Have all contract records been included in the ISO 26262 project archives?

1164. Change in attitude or behavior?

1165. Parties: Authorized?

1166. Has each contract been audited to verify acceptance and delivery?

1167. Have all contracts been closed?

1168. Change in knowledge?

1169. How does it work?

5.3 Project or Phase Close-Out: ISO 26262

1170. How often did each stakeholder need an update?

1171. What security considerations needed to be addressed during the procurement life cycle?

1172. Who exerted influence that has positively affected or negatively impacted the ISO 26262 project?

1173. What were the actual outcomes?

1174. What are the marketing communication needs for each stakeholder?

1175. Complete yes or no?

1176. What are the mandatory communication needs for each stakeholder?

1177. Is the lesson significant, valid, and applicable?

1178. What were the goals and objectives of the communications strategy for the ISO 26262 project?

1179. What hierarchical authority does the stakeholder have in your organization?

1180. Have business partners been involved extensively, and what data was required for them?

1181. Did the ISO 26262 project management methodology work?

1182. What are they?

1183. Is there a clear cause and effect between the activity and the lesson learned?

1184. What can you do better next time, and what specific actions can you take to improve?

1185. Who are the ISO 26262 project stakeholders and what are roles and involvement?

5.4 Lessons Learned: ISO 26262

1186. What is your strategy for data collection?

1187. How efficient and effective were ISO 26262 project team meetings?

1188. What was the methodology behind successful learning experiences, and how might they be applied to the broader challenge of your organizations knowledge management?

1189. What were the lessons learned on this ISO 26262 project?

1190. Was sufficient advance training conducted and/or information provided to enable the already stated affected by the changes to adjust to and accommodate them?

1191. What is the expected lifespan of the deliverable?

1192. How effective was the acceptance management process?

1193. Was the change control process properly implemented to manage changes to cost, scope, schedule, or quality?

1194. What are the Benefits of Measurements?

1195. What were the challenges and pitfalls?

1196. Were quality procedures built into the ISO

26262 project?

1197. What would you approach differently next time?

1198. Was the purpose of the ISO 26262 project, the end products and success criteria clearly defined and agreed at the start?

1199. What are the external dependencies?

1200. What is the supplier dependency?

1201. How well do you feel the executives supported this ISO 26262 project?

1202. Who managed most of the communication within the ISO 26262 project?

1203. How was the ISO 26262 project controlled?

1204. What are the internal dependencies?

1205. How to write up the lesson identified – how will you document the results of your analysis corresponding that you have an li ready to take the next step in the ll process?

Index

procedure   23, 111, 254, 264
procedures   11, 78, 86-88, 104, 145, 155, 160, 172, 176, 190, 217, 237, 250-251, 254, 269
proceeding   178, 181
process   4, 6-9, 11, 30, 32-34, 37, 40, 43, 45-46, 50-51, 53-55, 57-61, 63-69, 71, 77, 79, 82, 86-91, 94-95, 134, 141, 146, 148-149, 151, 153-156, 172, 176-177, 179, 181, 191, 194-195, 199, 201, 207-209, 215-216, 222, 227, 231, 235-237, 240, 242, 246, 251-252, 256, 259-260, 263, 269-270
processed   66
processes   1, 32, 58, 60-62, 64-66, 68, 87, 134, 162, 177, 191, 195, 197, 214, 218, 220, 222, 228, 233, 237, 246-247, 260
processor   66
procuring   160
produce   1, 172, 184, 224, 235
produced   73, 222
producing   151
product   3, 24, 27, 41, 48, 78, 81, 100, 103-104, 107-108, 111, 116, 121, 127, 137, 145, 168, 176, 188, 191, 193, 204-205, 212, 224-225, 236, 252-254, 258, 260
production   237, 263
products   3, 19, 59, 92, 127, 137, 141, 147, 152, 224, 229, 255, 270
profile 233
profit   193
program   18, 66, 74, 104, 141, 191, 198, 223, 233, 246
programme   119, 222
programs   129, 144, 225-226, 233, 262
progress   27, 75, 81, 89, 139, 186, 195, 218, 222, 249
prohibited   262
project 4-5, 7-10, 19, 30, 41, 54, 58, 64, 77, 86, 93, 95, 105, 107, 115, 117, 122, 124, 130, 133-136, 138-149, 151, 153-154, 156-157, 160, 162, 164-166, 168, 170-171, 174-189, 196, 198-201, 203-211, 214-215, 218-224, 228-229, 235-236, 246-250, 252, 254, 256, 258-261, 265, 267-270
projected   160, 196, 251
projects   4, 54, 94, 102-103, 107, 133, 135-136, 141-142, 144, 151, 153, 158, 177, 199, 207, 222, 224-225, 236-237, 252-253
promise   100
promote   58, 121
promotes   60
promotion   198
prompt   71

usability   101
useful   75, 92, 157, 177, 204
usefully 11, 18
usually 1
utility   178
utilizing 1, 78
validate   46, 114, 126, 252
validated   32-34, 64, 68
validation   42, 48, 81, 103, 109, 252
valuable   9
values 159, 199
variables   54, 90, 231
variance   7, 239, 241, 250-251
variances   159, 162, 250-251
variation   17, 32, 50-51, 53, 55, 59, 67, 89
various 214
vehicle 17, 35, 45, 51, 62, 65, 67, 69, 71, 73, 80, 83, 88, 96, 98-99,
101-104, 106, 108-111, 114-116, 120, 122-123, 125-126, 128-129,
131
vehicles   18, 20, 22, 24, 26, 37-38, 41-42, 47, 51, 54, 70, 85,
90, 94, 99-103, 105-107, 110-111, 114, 116, 118-120, 123-126, 128,
130-131
vendor 73, 135, 170, 214, 262
vendors   24, 63, 83, 153, 214, 262
verified 11, 32-34, 64, 100, 106, 109, 129
verify   46-47, 53, 55, 94, 153, 181, 253, 266
verifying   48, 154
Version 256, 271
versions   33, 37
versus   124
vested 212
viable 93
vibration   120
violate 38
violating   18
violations   155
visualize   165, 178
voices 138, 140
volatility   255
voluntary   91, 94
waited 2
walking   2
warrant   235

Printed in Great Britain
by Amazon

22043335R00176